Downtrodden
Abbey

THOMAS DUNNE BOOKS

ST. MARTIN'S PRESS 〰 NEW YORK

Downtrodden
Abbey

THE INTERMINABLE SAGA OF AN
INSUFFERABLE FAMILY

Gillian Fetlocks

THOMAS DUNNE BOOKS.

An imprint of St. Martin's Press.

DOWNTRODDDEN ABBEY. Copyright © 2013 by Billy Frolick. All rights reserved. Printed in the United States of America. For information, address St. Martin's Press, 175 Fifth Avenue, New York, N.Y. 10010.

www.thomasdunnebooks.com

www.stmartins.com

Library of Congress Cataloging-in-Publication Data

Fetlocks, Gillian.
  Downtrodden Abbey : the interminable saga of an insufferable family / Gillian Fetlocks.—First edition.
    pp. cm.
  Includes bibliographical references and index.
  ISBN 978-1-250-03123-5 (hardcover)
  ISBN 978-1-250-03124-2 (e-book)
  1. Downton Abbey (Television program)—Parodies, imitations, etc. 2. Upper class—England—Social life and customs—20th century—Fiction. 3. Household employees—Great Britain—Social life and customs—20th century—Fiction. I. Title.
  PR6106.E85D69 2013
  823'.92—dc23   2013023820

St. Martin's Press books may be purchased for educational, business, or promotional use. For information on bulk purchases, please contact Macmillan Corporate and Premium Sales Department at 1-800-221-7945, extension 5442, or write specialmarkets@macmillan.com.

First Edition: December 2013

10 9 8 7 6 5 4 3 2 1

FOR LADY FREDERICA HOBIN

"We have all read books that should never have been published. . . ."

CONTENTS

FOREWORD

It may be useful to begin with the great house itself.

The construction of Downtrodden Abbey was commissioned in 1659. The reputation of the architect, Inigo Schwartz, is still a subject of considerable debate. Depending on whom one believes, he was known for either unlimited patience or incessant dilly-dallying. For example, a small village originally occupied the land on which he planned to build. But as a courtesy—and in accordance with the etiquette of the day—Inigo Schwartz waited for every one of the residents to contract smallpox and expire before actually breaking ground. Would that such manners pervaded all of England's citizens in the Edwardian Age!

After waiting for the drafting table to be invented, the master designer generated plans for what was to be his crowning achievement: a dwelling massive enough to contain the secrets of the Earl of Grandsun and his descendants. In other words, the Earl of Grandsun's sons, daughters, grandsons, and grand-daughters. And the Earl of Grandsun's grandsons' sons and grandsons, and so forth.

Schwartz hired labourers to dig the foundation. Claiming a carriage failure on the way, they arrived two hours late, and immediately broke for lunch. However, as this was a fourteen-year project, they were forgiven. Masons eventually began to lay the stone; one enterprising and quite fortunate worker managed to do the same to Schwartz's fetching wife.

Fittingly, architect Inigo Schwartz' wife was built.

Finally, the structure was completed. In 1675, the first Earl of Grandsun moved into Downtrodden Abbey with his wife, who immediately took to bed, despondent over the colour of the drapes. Months later—as was common in that troubled era—this was reported as the official cause of her untimely death.

Electrical power came to the abbey in stages. Originally the first floor was electrified, then the bedrooms were electrified, and then the servants' quarters were electrified. (Lady Marry Crawfish, a later earl's eldest daughter, was electrified by the appearance of an Arab in her boudoir—but more on that later.)

As group clamouring was a popular activity of the day (according to Simon Potter's seminal study, *What's the Big Deal? Edwardian Group Clamouring and Its Consequences*, Dinder-Mufflin, 1931), visitors from all around the world clamoured to see the great house. These annoying gawkers would make drawings, take daguerrotype photographs, dance the popular "Downtrodden Jig" on the grounds of the estate, and colourfully describe the property in missives they sent back home.

"Yah, it is a most impressyve hoöse, one vich does not appear to have been put together from a kit," said the Swedish builder Allen Wrench.

"I wish my wife were built like this," wrote a comedian, who travelled to the abbey from Russia's Borscht Belt, ostensibly just to break out that old chestnut.

"What am I doing here?" asked the German neuropathologist Alois Alzheimer during his 1906 trip to Downtrodden.

"The abbey is both pleasing to the eye and functional," said an architectural writer of the day, who was known to occasionally lapse into overzealous hyperbole. "It is a towering

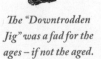

The "Downtrodden Jig" was a fad for the ages – if not the aged.

tribute to the wonders of modern industry, a marvel of design, and a triumph of the human spirit. Were it possible to engage in illicit acts of a carnal nature with a building, one would undoubtedly find Downtrodden Abbey a most suitable partner."

I. M. Hyly-Pade
Big-Time Architect

PREFACE

Let us now concern ourselves with some historical context for the story of this extraordinary house and its occupants.

Many do not realize that King Edward VII's reign was a scant nine years, beginning in 1901. Britain was a most ill-regarded country, in large part because the Boer War was still raging. Etymologists from every district waged battle in pubs over the correct spelling of the word "Boer," the early versions of which were "Bore" and "Boar." Fights broke out; many combatants died (ironically, of boredom). Others flourished in academia, where heavy alcohol consumption and protracted debate over utter nonsense has since been both encouraged and rewarded.

While the spelling over their name was being argued, the Boers kicked some serious limey posterior, as the British Army were cursed with overly thick uniforms, faulty sweat glands, and a collective lacklustre attitude. Rather than providing relief, occasional rain made the Conflict even more challenging for the British side, as the soldiers insisted on fighting whilst holding umbrellas.

In 1902, the Boer War ended. King Edward elected to test his questionable reputation with a cruise to Paris, and was disappointed to discover that he could not get a good table in a single decent restaurant. Nonetheless, upon his return to Blighty, the king delivered a series of speeches extolling the virtues of Paris, in an effort to restore good will between the nations. Aside from mistakenly referring to France's capital as "The Windy City," these upbeat talks did ultimately serve to bolster relations, particularly between the king and his French maid, Monique, who was aroused by any positive mention of her homeland.

Despite the strength of British imperialism in the years that followed, the disparity of the economic strata was cause for concern. While the wealthy held lavish parties in the gardens of grand estates and danced until dawn, the impoverished were only permitted to dance until seven or eight at night.

Many of the poor toiled as domestic servants, and due to the sheer number of them available in the workforce, they were paid

Domestic servants were hired to handle individual items of apparel, including one for each sock.

very little. Almost as revenge, these chefs, foot masseurs, and maids entertained themselves with gossip and transgressions against the expected behaviour of the day. As they had little or no money, they were immune to financial ruin, or accusations of slander. In some ways, they possessed more power than their employers.

However, they did have to eat slop, live in dumpy little rooms, and start work at five in the morning. So maybe "power" isn't the best word.

DRAMATIS PERSONAE

LORD RODERICK CRAWFISH, *Earl of Grandsun*

COUNTESS FLORA CRAWFISH, *his Yankee wife*

SURLY MCPAIN, *Flora's annoying mother*

LADY MARRY CRAWFISH, *their fetching daughter*

LADY SUPPLE CRAWFISH, *their even more fetching daughter*

LADY ENID CRAWFISH, *the daughter with the* personality,
 let's just say

VILE CRAWFISH, *Dowager Countess of Grandsun*

ATCHEW CRAWFISH, *third cousin of Lord Grandsun*

ISABICH CRAWFISH, *Atchew's mother*

SOLVENIA SWINE, *Atchew's fiancée*

DICK CALAMINE, *Lady Marry's suitor*

MRS. USED, *housekeeper*

TYRESOM, *butler*

LAIZY, *scullery maid*

EDSEL PARKS, *housemaid*

"POTATOES" O'Grotten, *Lady Flora's maid*

TOMAINE, *first footmasseur*

JOHN BRACE, *Lord Grandsun's valet*

VIRAL BRACE, *his wife*

NANA, *mousy housemaid*

MRS. PATMIMORE, *visually impaired, talent-compromised cook*

WREN, *housemaid/screenwriter*

JIGGY, *hot-ass footmasseur*

HIVY, *smokin' scullery maid*

HANDSOM, *Irish chauffeur/troublemaker*

JEN NEHSAYQUA, *Lithe, coltish maid*

CAMEL HOKKYPUK, *incontinent Arab*

HOWIE KREPLACH, *your basic Jew lawyer*

Part One

The First Part

That Sinking Feeling

It is the residents who occupy Downtrodden Abbey shortly after the turn of the twentieth century to whom we will now turn our attention.

The year is 1912—specifically, October the fifth—when word spreads that a telegramme is on its way.

"What is this 'telegramme' you speak of?" asks Vile, the dowager countess, who is so old that her eighth-grade science project was The Wheel. This woman's wrinkles have wrinkles, I wanna tell you.

"We've been through this countless times, Countess," responds Mrs. Used, the bitter, no-nonsense housekeeper. "The telegramme is one of the great conveniences of the modern era. A short message is written. Each character—letters and punctuation marks—is set on a printing press, and one edition of the message is produced. The page is then passed to a paid courier who—on horseback, seafaring vessel, or foot—journeys over mountain, sea, and sand. A mere three to six months later, it is delivered to the intended recipient's doorstep. One would be hard-pressed to find a more convenient or expeditious method of communication."

"This technology is simply out of hand," marvels Vile. "Whatever will they think of next?"

Mrs. Used explains that there is rumour of a version in which a strapping lad dressed as a bobby sings the telegramme's contents in celebration of a female's birthday or impending nuptials. But it turns out that the lad is not in actuality a bobby, and shortly after announcing his arrival he begins to disrobe, accompanied by saucy harpsichord music and the screams of the other female guests.

"Oh, Mrs. Used, it sounds like you've been in the wine cellar again," Vile says, wagging a gnarled finger. "Are you balmy on the crumpet, woman? I, for one, refuse to believe such hogwash prior to verifying it with the Snopes office."

Tonight, in the parlour, a game of Charades has been organised.

Lord Crawfish and his wife, Flora, will seize any opportunity to enjoy leisure games with their three daughters. However, following a croquet accident that left one of their uncles with a head injury and an insistence on permanently thereafter wearing an unsightly pith helmet and only speaking in Latin, these activities were limited to indoor, more cerebral pursuits.

A few words about Flora Crawfish. She eats poorly, reads trashy novels, is ignorant about politics and is unsophisticated

At the turn of the century, hormonally challenged girls were often armed with croquet mallets.

with language. When attending sporting events, she is bois-terous to the point of those around her requesting Security. She could spend weeks on a beach, drinking cheap wine, read-ing gossip magazines, and gambling on fixed dog races (in which both the dogs and the races are fixed) at night.

If you have not surmised it, Flora Crawfish is American.

Beautiful Lady Marry—the oldest Crawfish daughter—has skin like porcelain, but rest assured that in no other way does she resemble the accoutrements of tea service. For one thing, fine china could hardly withstand the bedroom acrobat-ics Lady Marry simply cannot live without. It is said that she has seen more ceilings than Michelangelo. For years, she has successfully managed to withhold knowledge of her insatiable appetite for fornication from her family. She keeps such ribald secrets between herself and her diary. A suffragette in theory if not practice, Lady Marry has for years been lobbying for hemlines to be lifted by one half inch.

Lady Supple, the youngest daughter, has silken tresses that frame a face of unutterable mystery. As might be expected, a woman this lovely could not possibly have a brain in her head, and Supple is no exception.

(Note: Women's figures in the twentieth century were—how to put this delicately?—smokin'. More zaftig than the Victorians, by the 1910s, women wore long corsets cut below the chest. Small animals, preferably deceased, were often inserted to exaggerate the size of the bosoms. When only living critters were available, ladies often resorted to the "Thingamajigger," a scooped-out melon half, stuffed with horsehair and attached to metal springs, all of which were anchored by a frame of human bone. Adverts for bust cream peppered periodicals of the day. These magic potions allegedly create "That Va-va-vavoom Effect," and guaranteed "Staggering Bulges from All Passing Gents." Chinese tinctures were also quite popular, but an hour after application, they had to be applied again.)

The Crawfishes know nothing of Supple's hidden desire: to locate and wed the most destitute Irishman in the county and endure an impoverished existence of resentment, hardship, and impassioned political belief.

Lastly and very much leastly there is Lady Enid, the middle child, who in private regularly curses nature for the wrath it unleashed on her. She is distinguished by inordinately large knuckles, load-bearing hips, and a facial expression less reminiscent of the *Mona Lisa* than of *The Scream*. But to quote the Duke of Flashingmore following a crushing defeat on the polo pitch in Oxford, "One cannot win them all." Enid, too, has secrets, but no one is terribly interested in them.

It is on Enid's tragically unfortunate countenance, however, that her family's eyes are presently trained. She reads a clue and begins to pantomime its contents, starting by extending her arms, one on either side of her not inconsiderable, highly asymmetrical frame.

"Big!" Lord Grandsun surmises, but Enid shakes her head laterally as she continues to silently act.

"Grand!" his wife Flora guesses, which is also followed by a negative response.

"Girth!" yells Lady Marry confidently. But she, too, is incorrect.

Enid again glances at the clue, then alters her strategy. She plummets her hands, as though suddenly submerging them in water.

"'Diving'?" Lady Supple queries.

"'Plunging'?" offers Flora.

"I know, I know," says Marry, excitedly. "It's—it's 'going down' . . ."

Enid nods with enthusiasm, pointing with a crooked index finger to her deformed nose.

"Going down . . . would it be 'Fellatio' . . . ?"

Flora blushes crimson. "Marry!"

"Hear me out, mother, I think I've got the answer," Marry

continues. "Could it be 'A well-endowed Arab found in my boudoir'?"

The shocked silence that follows is broken by the disgusted Lord Grandsun.

"Marry Crawfish! Wherever would you conjure such an appalling image?"

His eldest shrugs, questioning to herself the wisdom of having imbibed her third cognac.

Flora stands conclusively. "In my opinion, this game is concluded," she concludes.

"Is no one curious as to the correct answer?" Lady Enid asks. "It was 'The Sinking of the *Gigantic*.'"

Lady Supple giggles. "Oh, pul-*ease*. Like that could ever happen."

Mrs. Used appears in the doorway, telegramme in hand.

"Lord Crawfish," she says, handing him the water-damaged document. "I forgot to give you this the other day."

TELEGRAMME

DATED: APRIL 16, 1912
TO: LORD RODERICK CRAWFISH, EARL OF GRANDSUN
FROM: LANE CRAWFISH

UPDATING OUR GIGANTIC CRUISE. STOP. FOOD IS TERRIBLE. STOP. AND SUCH SMALL PORTIONS. STOP. LOST A SMALL FORTUNE IN THE CASINO. STOP. TEE SHIRTS AND SOUVENIRS WAY OVERPRICED. STOP. NIGHTLY "ENTERTAINMENT" CONSISTS OF SEMITIC YANK MOTORMOUTH CALLED JOAN RIVERS. SHORT CAREER

PREDICTED. STOP. SHIP IS UNEXPECTEDLY HEADED STRAIGHT FOR OBSCURE COUNTRY CALLED "ICE-BERG," NAME OF WHICH CREW IS SHOUTING LOUDLY AND REPEATEDLY. STOP. PLEASE CHECK AT MY HOME TO SEE IF I LEFT FURNACE ON. JUST HAVE THAT SINK-ING FEELING. STOP.

REGARDS

LANE

Lord Grandsun's face registers profound concern.

"Evidently, it's true," he tells his family. "The fact that this telegramme is actually soaking wet is not a good sign. Clearly, the *Gigantic* has sunk. And so, in turn, are we. I assume you all know about the entail."

Enid stands, again attracting the attention of the others.

"Of course. The entail is one of a human or animal's intestines or internal organs, especially when removed or exposed."

"Enid . . ." Flora pleads, to no avail, as her homely offspring continues.

"These are also known as the bowels, guts, viscera, or innards."

Lord Grandsun rolls his eyes. "Not 'entrails,' Enid. I said 'entail.'"

"Oh—I think I know," Enid offers excitedly. "Would that be the end of an animal's tail?"

Marry can take no more of her sister's idiocy. "Crikey, Enid—now you're merely guessing. The charades game is over, remember? Please let Father continue."

Lord Grandsun explains the consequences of the ship sinking in as succinct terms as possible: Roderick's nephew Pettrick was to marry Marry, his oldest daughter, thus inheriting the title and fortune tied to the property from Flora, Marry's American mother. According to the entail, the land and title must pass to a male heir.

If there are two things the earl despises, they are moving and going belly up, both of which seem in the offing. For a minute he wonders if Enid could pass for a man, which, from a cosmetic standpoint, is a feat that could be easily executed. But then she would have to marry her own sister, which would undoubtedly present additional problems, heir-wise.

Marry, meanwhile, must feign sorrow over the loss of her intended, who in truth had an unfortunate twitch and the breath of an ailing bison. She puts her head in her hands and sobs.

"Marry, you're not exactly posing a threat to the Barrymores with that performance," Enid scoffs. "I've seen better acting in grade-school pageants."

"Snap!" Supple's corset pops open, inexplicably.

Lord Crawfish's solicitor visits, tells him that the entail is unbreakable, and—adding insult to injury—it being the weekend, he charges the earl double for his time. The lawyer also spends most of their meeting bragging about his new carriage, and his young mistress, whom he met while she was helping to deliver his first child. Upon learning of this, Flora surmises that the attorney is going through "a midwife crisis."

Downstairs, "Potatoes" O'Grotten, Lady Crawfish's maid, mutters. She is an expert mutterer, having been trained at an early age. Her mother muttered, and her mother's mother muttered. O'Grotten's audience is her usual confidant, the first footmasseur

*Poorly endowed men were known to boast about
the size of their carriage wheels.*

Tomaine. Tomaine has been working diligently on perfecting his bitterness and resentment; it is frequently noted around the abbey that he can smoke without even lighting a cigarette. When he is not smoking, Tomaine mutters, and O'Grotten takes over the smoking.

Tomaine's mood is not lifted in the slightest by the arrival of a motorcar containing John Brace, who is to be employed as the earl's personal valet (parking and otherwise).

Lord Crawfish watches from upstairs as Brace gets out of the car and starts the fifty-metre walk towards the front entrance. Brace's first step goes reasonably well, but it is rather rough sailing from that point. Offered assistance by one of the foot-masseurs, he smiles, assuring them that he will reach the house before sundown.

Sadly, it is just after eight in the morning when Brace says this.

When Brace finally does get himself into the hallowed halls of Downtrodden Abbey, dinner has been served, the kitchen has been cleaned, and the staff—particularly O'Grotten and Tomaine—are most eager to make his acquaintance.

"Welcome to the Abbey," O'Grotten mutters, blowing a healthy cloud of smoke into his doughy face.

"Aren't you a breath of fresh air?" Brace asks, not at all rhetorically.

"How was your, er, *trip*?" asks Tomaine. "It seems to have started last . . . um, *fall*. Guess you just have to *take everything in stride*." He elbows O'Grotten in the ribs, a habit she detests.

(It is worth noting that Tomaine—how best to say this?— has a deep love of theatre, particularly of the musical variety. Some of his gesticulations and mannerisms might occasionally strike one as extravagant, showy, or overly flamboyant. Tomaine is also known to wear ladies' clothing and makeup. But his father was never really there for him, his mother ran a backroom billiard hall fronted by a convent, and his older brothers were fond of quizzing the young Tomaine on the rules of cricket, and—following his incorrect answers—would beat him mercilessly. After a one-man show in which Tomaine played Sarah Bernhardt got drubbed by West End critics, he allegedly turned to opium, then engaged in a tryst with both Currier and Ives that ended in nothing but hurt feelings.)

"Well, I would advise you to brace yourself, Brace," mutters O'Grotten. "This is no job for a . . . crip—uh . . ."

"Pardon me, Madam?"

"A Crimean!" Tomaine exclaims. "I'm picking up a little, something in your patois . . . not to mention those deep-set eyes, and that swarthy complexion. . . ."

"I'm Liverpool born and bred. Watch who you call a Crimean, son."

Around the corner, the teen-aged housemaid Nana surreptitiously peeks at Brace. She has spent countless shillings on some of the local mating services ("Edwardian Hook Up," "Gents Plus Damsels," "Ripping Bodices"), only to be regularly disappointed. These fellows are all the same, she has discovered. It seems that surprisingly few gentlemen covet a young lady who spends an inordinate amount of time in the company of soiled bedclothes, despite the necessity of such contact in her chosen profession.

Also quite troubling regarding the mating services is that every man in reality is three stones heavier and fifteen years older than his charcoal sketch. Having only four hours of discretionary time per week also

The phrase "Losing one's leg" was sometimes taken literally by the unfortunate but optimistic souls who searched for missing limbs.

makes Nana's social life rather challenging. She has considered changing her profile, but the mail delivery is dreadfully slow.

In short, the greatest fear for this young maid is—you guessed it—becoming an old maid.

In John Brace, however, Nana immediately sees the possibilities. He seems to be right up her street—overweight, elderly, acne-scarred, and emotionally damaged. Even the two hours it takes Brace to walks upstairs does not deter her. After all, "putting one foot in front of the other" is just a metaphor, she thinks, nothing to interpret literally. Nana is smitten.

"I'll bet he's not 'limp' where it matters," she coos softly. "That bloke can butter my scones any time."

"I heard that," smirks Tomaine from behind her.

"That was meant to be a silent coo."

"Well, it came out as a soft one. So I'd work on my cooing, if I were you. In any event, whatever would you want with a pudgy, long-in-the-tooth gimp unless you have some, like, serious daddy issues?"

Nana sighs. Some people just have no concept of true love.

Lord Crawfish, in his quarters, is pleased to receive his old mate Brace. The timing could not be better, as the inconvenient business of putting on his own pajamas, coats, and trousers has of late been distressing the earl.

As he watches Brace's gait, however, the question of the new valet's future instantly comes into bold relief. Physical movement from the waist down seems, for Brace, to require an intricate meshing of mental cues and Newtonian physics.

"Brace," Lord Crawfish asks, "Can I ask you something?"

"Certainly, my Lord," Brace answers, as he readies his employer's pants for the insertion of the aristocratic limbs.

"What in the name of Kaiser Fodder has happened to you?"

"Lost my right leg, I have."

"Have you looked everywhere?"

Brace chuckles. "Clearly one thing that has *not* been lost is your wicked sense of humour, my lord. In fact, it seems even sharper. Have you, by chance, been spending time with individuals of the Jewish persuasion?"

"Oh, heavens, no. We at the Abbey do not consort with Semites."

Brace sighs with approval.

The following day brings a visit from the Viscount of Crowsfeces, with the express purposes of catching Lady Marry's eye, or even more preferably, her royal bosom. Or, in the perfect world, both bosoms, actually. For it was as her husband that he would become the next Earl of Grandsun. The bosoms would really just be a bonus.

(It should be explained that in this society, marriages are often arranged by parents and attorneys, in an effort to combine the financial assets of both families. The lawyers often end up more wealthy than their clients, a tradition that continues to this day.)

The Viscount requests Tomaine as his footmasseur; he is all too willing—as he is with most positions—to assume this one. Prior to starting his duties, though, he strategically places a skateboard on the floor of the vestibule. After breakfast,

*For the servants, schlepping heavy tea service up and down steep
staircases was an absolute pain the ass.*

this sends Brace—and a tray of tea service—toppling to the
ground.

"I meant to do that!" Brace smiles, felled by lack of balance
but propelled by pride, as the shocked staff and the horrified
Viscount look on.

"Brace, this is no line of work for a gimp. Regretfully, I
have no choice but to dismiss you," says Lord Crawfish. "I'll
give you two weeks. Which should give you just enough time
to navigate the front steps and permanently exit the grounds of
Downtrodden Abbey."

Later, Nana finds Brace outside, his bags packed, weeping
near the rose bushes.

"Mr. Brace, you left something inside," she says.

"Mind cranking up the volume a notch?" Brace asks, pointing to his left ear. "As if I don't have enough problems, I had a
recent bout with the pox of the chicken, which resulted in
some hearing loss."

The mere mention of another of Brace's limitless maladies

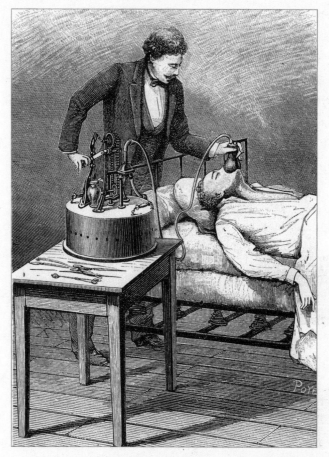

*A doctor's main responsibility to the infirm was to attach them
to rusted, filthy, unsafe contraptions.*

arouses Nana's naughty bits. "Well, *I* certainly want to hear—all
about your allergies, infections, diseases, illnesses, and the general decrepitude that comes with advanced age. It all gets my
blood flowing."

"Really? I'm nothing if not envious. Blood circulation is another problem for me."

Nana's bodice is fit to bursting. "Iron deficiency? You really know what to say to a lass, mister."

Brace is gobsmacked by this level of female attention. However, one question remains unanswered.

"To what were you referring when you said I left something back in the Abbey?" he asks.

"You silly old man," she coos—this time, loud enough for the velveteen valet to hear. "It's your heart."

"Speaking of my heart," Brace says. "That's not great, either. I got infarctions up the ying-yang."

After breaking bread (and wind), Viscount Crowsfeces breaks protocol, by persuading Lady Marry to show him the servant's sleeping area, where he takes a special interest in Tomaine's quarters.

"Any particular reason you are sniffing around his undergarments?" she asks.

"I can tell you one thing," Crowsfeces responds. "It is not because we shared a summer dalliance on the shores of Cornwall, or because I miss his lively dancing and sweet scent so dearly, or because there is anything about me that would cause you to doubt my ability to both bed you like a bull and make you a fine husband."

Lady Marry explains her father's decision not to challenge the entail.

"I see," says the Viscount, realizing now that courting Marry would be a fool's errand. "In that case, do you happen to know where I might find my man?"

A NOTE FROM THE AUTHOR

It would be foolish to believe that the average reader can grasp the concept of British nobility—that is to say, how titles are conferred and their order (particularly American readers, and especially those homeschooled in the South). Of course, British children "to the manor born" are taught early on that snobbishness, condescension, and arrogance are birthrights, designed for one to feel superior, and to make others feel inadequate and impoverished. But for those of us who are not lords or ladies (and you know who you are), I have gone to great lengths to prepare the following guide.

DUKE
Though this is the highest rank and title, a duke wears a coronet rather than a crown. The decoration on the coronet is two diamond eyes looking down a bulbous pearl nose, on a bed of tea cakes made of emeralds. A duke is usually addressed as "Most Noble," except in cases when "Quite Noble," "Rather Noble," or "Somewhat Noble" are more accurate. His children's titles are preceded by "Right Honourable"—sons are "lords," daughters are "ladies," and rare cases of indeterminate gender are "undecided." As they all wear ruffled shirts, who can tell? Later bastardised as the nickname for an American cowboy actor,

and by the insufferable expression "Put up your dukes," which makes no sense whatsoever, in that most dukes are extremely well-fed, and far too portly to lift, let alone "put up."

MARQUESS/MARQUIS

Just below the duke in British peerage ranks the marquis, whose young sons use the title "lord," but rarely put it back where they found it. Elder sons bear the father's second title. Daughters are "ladies," whether or not they comport themselves accordingly. Eventually appropriated by the Yanks for the name of an unsightly model of Mercury automobile.

EARL

The third level of dignity and rank, the earl is titled "Right Honourable" by everyone except his wife, who will be damned before she ascribes either quality to her spouse. Midwestern Americans use "Earl" as a common first name, while a hit song in 1962 entitled "Duke of Earl" served to confuse those who were already perplexed about title hierarchy even further.

VISCOUNT

If one is a viscount, one is probably dealing with some self-esteem issues, as many of your friends are earls, marquises, and dukes. Oh, well. Look at the bright side. At least one is not a . . .

BARON

The lowest rank in the British peerage. Serious losers.

II

A Real Head Scratcher

It is said that at one time or another Downtrodden Abbey hosted not just noblemen, but high-profile guests from all corners of the world (this was, it should be explained, a time in which the world was believed to actually have corners). Selected notations from the guest register, as entered by the butler, Tyresom, follow:

CHARLES CHAPLIN—AUGUST 12–14, 1912
May be silent in motion pictures, but at dinner hardly shuts up. Pays special attention to young housemaids, and refers to his "cane" frequently, as a nickname for the male organ. Mustache is curiously Germanic.

AMELIA EARHART—OCTOBER 5–6, 1912

Definite lesbian vibe. Blathers incessantly about something called "The Bermuda Triangle," which sounds suspiciously like a euphemism for a part of the female anatomy. Tends to disappear at times, particularly when it is her turn to buy drinks.

MOHANDAS "MAHATMA" GANDHI—MARCH 8–17, 1913

I don't care what anyone tells you—this guy can really eat. Keep him away from the dessert cart. Evidently, Mr. Brace isn't the only one around here with a hollow leg. Gasses on incessantly about the importance of peace, but try getting him to surrender the last "piece" of chocolate cake.

The expression "Look at the size of those jugs!" originally referred to surprisingly large beverage containers.

WINSTON CHURCHILL—MAY 28, 1913

Attacks from both fronts with chronic gastritis and horrendous cigar breath. Cheats at Parcheesi, then—when victorious—gloats by making obnoxious sign with his index and middle fingers.

In Manchestershireburghville, Lord Crawfish's distant cousin Isabich receives a letter.

"Atchew," she beckons her only son. "How would like to be rolling in money and living in a lavish estate?"

Atchew, a strapping lad in his early twenties, shrugs. "What's the catch?"

"You'd have to marry one of the Crawfish girls," Isabich responds. "And I don't think it's the one with the face like a palamino."

"Well, you read my mind on that score. Uh, can I think about it?"

Preparations for guests at the Abbey involve considerable effort not just from servants but from Countess Flora, who assigns bedrooms and works with the cook, Mrs. Patmimore. To make things just a little bit more pretentious, menus are often written in French.

A year after the sinking of the *Gigantic* took the lives of the expected heirs to Downtrodden Abbey, Isabich and Atchew arrive at the estate and settle in.

Unfamiliar with the customs of the fabulously wealthy, Atchew readies himself for dinner, dressing in white tie. Fortunately, he is stopped by the butler, Tyresom, and informed that "white tie" is not to be taken literally, and that Atchew must wear additional clothing, especially trousers.

As the wine is poured, Isabich is seated next to Vile, the dowager countess of Grandsun.

"Excuse me," Isabich asks, "Are you alive?"

"How amusing," the countess counters. "From a woman who is probably thanked in the Acknowledgements section of the Holy Bible."

"Are you saying I'm advanced in age? I would venture to say that you are so old that when you were in grammar school, there was no History class. Now *that* is old."

The countess burns. "It is my understanding that you wandered into an antiques shop—*and they kept you.*"

"Really? Oh, do tell me, Countess—how did you get here? I'm guessing it was on a boat with two of every type of animal."

It should be mentioned that in these heady times, the wealthy do little else than eat. Seven meals a day are consumed: early breakfast, breakfast, teatime, late teatime, supper, early dinner, and late dinner. Most meals contain between twenty-one and twenty-three courses. Twenty-two, to be exact. Watercress is the old arugula. Oysters are often served as starters. Mutton is regularly featured as an entrée. Salmon is another popular choice. As for crabs, many of the residents and staff at Downtrodden Abbey unfortunately suffer from them.

Across the table, Atchew struggles to decide which of the nine forks in his setting he should employ to eat his salad. When he looks up, Lady Marry has entered the dining hall, and approaches the empty seat next to him.

*The ability to properly identify cutlery was considered
a benchmark of elegance.*

"Hubba hubba," Atchew gasps.

"I beg your pardon?"

"You . . . look lovely, Lady Marry."

Tomaine and O'Grotten look on from behind a pillar. "Can you believe that moron?" the latter whispers. "Does he really think he has a chance with Marry?"

"Why would you care?" O'Grotten asks. "Tsk. Such a bitchy little gossip you are, Tomaine. Considered along with the ease with which you carry a show tune and your inarguably smashing fashion sense, I am starting to suspect that you might be a homosexual."

Back in their modest residence, Atchew asks Isabich to explain the intricacies of what an entail exactly . . . entails.

"It is all very simple," his mother responds. "An entail is an estate of inheritance in real property that cannot be sold, devised by will, or otherwise be alienated by the owner, but which passes by operation of law to the owner's heirs upon his death. The purpose of an entail is to keep the land of a family intact in the main line of succession. The heir to an entailed estate cannot sell the land, nor usually bequeath it to, for example, an illegitimate child.

"It's also important to note that the explanation of an entail is a common device used in British drama taking place from the seventeenth to the nineteenth centuries, so as to keep the plot moving forwards and devious machinations understandable to the audience, be it reader or theatregoer. Also—"

She notices that her son has not responded in over half an hour.

"Atchew? Are you asleep?"

A few hours later, Vile pays an unscheduled visit to Isabich in her garden, with the intent to offer her an olive branch.

"What is this thing you keep poking me with?" asks Isabich.

"It's an olive branch. Sorry. My intent was merely to offer it, not poke you with it. Are you familiar with the reference? The poet Virgil used the olive branch as a symbol of peace in *Aeneid*. 'High on the stern Aeneas his stand, and held a branch of olive in his hand.'"

"So, you knew Virgil, did you?"

"Come on, Isabich. Can we stop with the 'you're so old' jokes? I mean, when you were born, the Dead Sea was just getting sick. Gosh, being nasty is quite addictive. It's like opium for geriatrics."

"Tell me about it."

Vile explains that she feels this is an opportune day to sit outside rather than within the confines of Downtrodden, as rumours have abounded that the house is being fitted for the dreaded electricity. Next thing you know, she surmises, there will be big screens that present video signals, and an international communication matrix with which—for a small fee—individuals will be able to expose their genitalia, reunite with former grade-school paramours, and be offered financial windfalls by Nigerian princes.

"Sit down, Vile," Isabich says. "You are talking like an utter madwoman."

Over tea and biscuits, Vile outlines her internal conflict. She finds Atchew to be a philistine, a knuckle-dragger, a caveman, a fop, a boob, and a dunderhead. And these are his positive qualities. The idea of him inheriting Downtrodden Abbey, with his inability to select the proper eating utensils, positively nauseates Vile. As do the very biscuits they are consuming, which taste like they have been designated for Fallow, Lord Crawfish's prized Chihuahua-Mastiff mix.

"However," says Vile, "There is the matter of my continuing to live in the style to which I have been accustomed. I cannot imagine my family not having ten times more house than they need, sumptuous meals, and a staff of white slaves we can criticize and berate day and night. It would simply be torture, I tell you.

"So I will reluctantly allow your dim-witted progeny to marry . . . Marry."

Back at the Abbey, however, Marry contemplates the idea of tying the knot for money rather than love. The whole business with the forks was certainly an indicator of what might develop out of a marriage to Atchew.

It's so simple, she thinks, sitting at her vanity. *There are nine forks. The smallest ones are for shellfish and escargot. The slightly larger one is for the first starter. The next is for the salad. The medium fork is for the second starter. The other medium fork is for the second salad. The large fork is for the main course. Wait—is that eight or nine? Did I miss one? This is the issue with men—they set one's head to spinning.*

Flora enters and, seeing her daughter's confusion, tries to help.

"Marry."

"Yes, mother?"

"That's all. I meant it as a verb this time."

"But how can I wed this man, mother? We have virtually no history."

Flora shares her memories. When she married Roderick she was hardly in love. He was prone to missing belt loops and failing to lift his little finger when sipping tea. Not to mention his problem in the boudoir (which was eventually solved with a blue potion provided by Mr. Stiffdick, the town apothecary).

"Okay, first of all, you're oversharing. And secondly, it's not Atchew's manhood I'm questioning—it is his manners. I mean, who eats pudding with a fork? And besides, I've got a viscount coming."

"A discount? Why would you need that, Marry? There is virtually nothing you cannot afford—especially as you are poised to inherit—"

"Mother, please. Clean the wax from yours ears. I said 'viscount.'"

Sneaking a minute to read the morning paper, Mr. Brace is enticed by an advert:

CRIPPLES WANTED!

Do you pull your leg around like Quasimodo after a long night out with the boys? When you walk downstairs, does it sound like you are dragging a dead body? Are you attempting to work as a valet at a massive estate, but continually bothered by the snickering of contemptible co-workers from behind, as one sort of girly fellow angling for your position seems determined to get your sorry rump sacked?

Something in the posting rings true for Brace—though he is not sure exactly what. At his earliest convenience, he makes an appointment in the village to see the advert's author, Dr. Mark Quidusade.

In the waiting room, Brace peruses the current issue of *Mallet & Saddle* to see how his fantasy fox hunting team is faring this week. Last place, as usual. Glad he couldn't afford season tickets. *Oh, well,* he thinks—*wait 'til next year.*

"Mr. Brace? The doctor will see you now," the receptionist calls out.

An hour later, Brace has filled out the necessary forms and—barely—lugs himself into Quidusade's office.

Once there he sees, on the wall, a huge metal device featuring sawteeth, barbs, sharp edges, clasps, and traps.

"Ironic and postmodern," Brace observes, as the doctor takes the contraption off of its hook. "How ingenious—a guillotine! A medieval torture device no doubt in view to settle the nerves of your patients, who would never have to endure such—pardon me, why are you putting that thing on my leg?"

"Mr. Brace. First off, one could hardly call this mangled flesh at the end of your torso a 'leg,'" Dr. Quidusade says. "I must urge you to allow me to do my work. It's very simple. I'll give you a shot of Scotch, then spend the next seven hours screwing this doohickey into whatever shred of bone you have left. Then all you have to do is get yourself accustomed to hauling around an extra four stones on the lower half of one side of your body."

"You're pulling my leg?"

Quidusade nods his head. "Indeed—pulling it, stretching it, manhandling and further misshaping it as well—"

"I meant, 'Are you jesting?'"

"I'm afraid not, old bean."

"Hmm . . ." Brace conjects. "I suppose it all sounds reasonable enough. One prays the Scotch is quite good."

Across town, another medical procedure is called for.

Isabich pays a visit to the Scalp Ward of Merciless Hospital, where she meets a young father suffering from chronic eczema, seborrhea, and—most poignantly—the heartbreak of psoriasis.

"Have you changed shampoos?" she asks the man, who is well beyond frustrated from the effects of constant itching.

"How can a fellow with such little hair suffer such hideous dandruff?" asks a voice from behind Isabich. It is Vile, as usual unable to keep her noble nose out of anyone else's affairs. The dowager countess questions Isabich's actions.

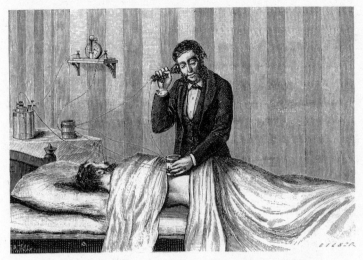

"The good news, sweetheart, is that I'll be home sooner than I thought."

"My dear Mrs. Crawfish. You cannot possibly hope to heal the world of its scalp problems. Seriously, how could one?"

"Balls," Isabich replies.

"Well, it certainly appears that you have no shortage of those."

"I mean *charity* balls, you senile witch. That's my plan to raise money and awareness of maladies of the pate. Additionally, it's not impossible—as Atchew is to inherit Downtrodden Abbey—that I would convert the entire structure into a clinic for the follically challenged. Offering not just scalp treatments, but possibly hair weaves, and waxing . . . perhaps a combination of hospital and high-end salon."

"Over my dead body!" Vile exclaims.

"That certainly sounds like a viable option. And if that's what it takes, I'll put a dagger into that crusty heel of bread you call your heart. Sorry. That came out a little harsher than I meant."

Vile shakes it off. "In any event, are there not more pressing problems in the world than dryness and flaking on the head? Smallpox, perhaps? Bubonic plague? The black death?"

Little does Vile know Isabich's secret—that her late husband's cause of death was severe, accelerated male pattern baldness. It has softened her, and afforded her a much greater sense of empathy and tenderness.

"Mind your own business, you old bat," Isabich snarls tenderly.

Snooping in the closet of a housemaid, Wren, a wrapped package intrigues Tyresom. Finally, he can stand it no longer, and he confronts her.

"It is a book," Wren confides. "On . . . how to write screenplays."

She explains that it is her fervent desire to create scenarios for motion pictures.

"That Chaplin gentleman who stayed here last summer encouraged me greatly. He claimed I had a natural ear for dialogue, and that he thoroughly enjoyed my story presentations. He firmly believed they were interesting enough for him to perform in someday. He also promised to introduce me to the head of a studio."

"Is there anything you are leaving out?" Tyresom asks.

"Oh, yes. Then he screwed me and told me he was in love with me. Though he left without saying goodbye or leaving a tip."

Tyresom has heard tales of the picture industry, and wonders if his young colleague knows what she is getting herself into.

"It all sounds well and good now, Wren. But from what I understand, the picture business is one in which canines eat canines. What happens when your agent fails to answer your letters?"

"All I know is, screenwriters must receive better treatment than maids . . . don't they?"

"I wouldn't count on it."

Tyresom confides in Wren that back in the day he plied the screenplay trade himself, despite (a) that motion pictures had not yet been invented, and (b) his parents' protestations that he take up any other line of work before writing, including selling himself down by the docks.

When the time came for him to file his application for the butler position at Downtrodden Abbey, Tyresom knew that he must keep his sordid past a secret.

Still, he does have a couple of projects he is developing, if one is ever interested in sitting down and hearing them.

RULES OF APPROPRIATE BEHAVIOUR IN THE EDWARDIAN AGE

At the Table

Mustachioed gentlemen should avoid the consumption of soup, as the likelihood of one doing so in an effective manner that does not nauseate his fellow diners is quite slim.

Mustachioed women are requested not to order soup either, or to appear in public in the first place. Mustachioed children should be brought to a physician.

Eating quickly is encouraged, as there are seven meals served each day. Slurping and chomping are the simplest ways to force food down the gullet.

Months after the meal in question, it was commonplace for gentlemen to find remnants in their beards.

Sliced bread should be no thicker than the guests at the table.

Women's Rights (and Wrongs)

A good hostess shakes hands with her guests, unless said guests do not have hands, in which case an alarmed stare is considered acceptable.

The hemline of a woman's dress should be high enough for a medium-sized mouse to walk under, but low enough to deter an adult possum from the same pursuit.

Women with mice and possum problems should not be concerned with the length of their hemlines, and instead be taking measures to rectify their pest issues.

Mice and possum wearing dresses should only be found in Beatrix Potter books. Women finding rodents in human clothing should not encourage this practice.

The wearing of rodent costumes by women should be limited to school holiday pageants.

Couture

When choosing to wear ostrich feathers in the hair, women should make certain that the ostrich in question is not still attached.

Men wearing ostrich feathers may experience public humiliation. Ostrich feathers should be secreted inside the trousers, which will produce a pleasant, and quite possibly arousing, sensation.

Gentlemen

Cheating at gin rummy is considered grounds for caning, whilst cheating in one's marriage, if done surreptitiously, is perfectly allowable. Go figure.

Singing and whistling on city streets is a punishable offense.

Parlourmaids often shirked their duties by throttling one another in the halls.

Excessive whining is considered a misdemeanour. Shrill catcalls are allowed at cockfights, but—interestingly—not at cat shows. Passing gas in church is thought to be rude and frowned upon, whilst passing the hat is always permissible.

Walking with the hands in the pockets is considered to be in poor taste, especially if the pockets in question do not belong to the owner of the hands.

Servants

Parlourmaids and manservants should never be thanked or complimented, as such comments invariably encourage complacency. The following terms should be used when turning a critical eye: *boob, stooge, idiot, cretin, sapsucker, moron, clown, worm, weasel, dummy,* and *arse-hole.*

III

An Unfortunate Leak

Hunting squirrels is considerably more challenging than fox hunting or shooting at pheasants and grouses. It is widely held that anyone can bag a deer or a duck—but only a true man can nail a cute rodent with a bushy tail.

A proper squirrel hunt has been organised on the grounds of Downtrodden Abbey, with a guest list that includes Estelle—yes, it is a man's name, believe it or not—Napster, who has brought along a dear friend.

He is a dashing Arab named Camel (clearly his parents had a wicked sense of humour). Tomaine is assigned to be his foot-masseur—a task he is only too pleased to undertake after getting a gander at the handsome Middle Easterner. In this rare instance, however, Tomaine does his job a bit *too* well, incurring the wrath of Camel, who becomes spitting mad.

Just before breakfast, Tomaine confides to O'Grotten the details of his failed tryst with Camel—unfiltered, as usual. O'Grotten's beady eyes nearly jump out of her sweat-soaked head.

"So let me get this straight," she says. "You attempted to hump Camel?"

"Exactly," Tomaine admits. "And within seconds, Camel was smoking. But it looks as though I am the one who got burned."

The plethora of camel-related wordplay exhausts O'Grotten, who needs to go and supervise the serving of breakfast.

The morning meal at Downtrodden Abbey is indeed a glorious affair. At seven o'clock sharp pots of India tea are served, along with a choice of pheasant, grouse, partridge, or ptarmigan. Anyone who can tell the difference between these inedible fowl is given an extra cup of tea. This is followed by biscuits and tea, tea and biscuits, and then another round of tea. The meal is capped off with tea all around, as well as biscuits.

Marry sits between Camel and Atchew, who is again flummoxed by the array of silverware before him. But tonight it is the handsome Arab who has her full attention.

"How do you like your sausage?" she asks him, perhaps a bit too loudly.

"You should try it some time," he replies. "And I am foreign, by the way—not deaf."

"Marry, would you use this spoon or that one to penetrate this melon?" asks Atchew.

How disgusting, she thinks. Using double entendre—what an amateur seduction tactic. She directs her focus back to Camel.

"I'd love to sample your sausage," Marry purrs. "Maybe in my boudoir, later tonight."

"Are you saying what I think you are?" Camel asks. "Eating in one's bedroom is not frowned upon at Downtrodden? And breakfast fare—in the evening?"

He's not very bright, Marry thinks, *but I would definitely give this Camel a ride.*

That night, the Arab is anything but deserted, as he makes his way into Marry's bedroom.

"Why, Camel," Marry exclaims. "Don't tell me you've come here for a bit of the old slap-and-tickle?"

"What?" he asks.

"The old slap-and-tickle? Shagging. Making whoopee. Rolling in the hay. The horizontal bop. The monster with two backs. El Schtuppo. Hide the salami. The Venus Fly Trap. Intercourse. Bumping uglies. Doing the Dirty. Sticking it in. The Hot Beef Injection. Banging. Laying pipe. Cattle prodding the oyster ditch. Marinating the nether rod in the squish mitten. Retrofitting the pudding hatch with the boink swatter.

"And I could go on."

"Evidently you can," says Camel. "That is quite a vocabulary you have there. But the truth is, much as I would enjoy mitten-bumping—or whatever you want to call it—this morning's squirrel hunt has absolutely flattened me. I am simply exhausted, and my mattress is lumpier than Mrs. Patmimore's porridge."

So that is his agenda, Marry thinks. *Camel is just using me for my comfortable mattress. How dare this despicable sand merchant assume that he can take advantage of me!*

"Come on in," Marry says.

"Can I just run to the loo?"

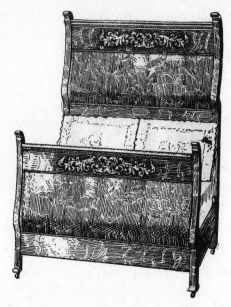

Midget bed, c. 1916.

"I, uh, wouldn't go in there for a while," she advises. "That boiled squab we had for dinner really did a number on me."

Two hours later, Marry makes a tragic discovery, races down the hall to Nana's quarters, and knocks on the door.

"Mr. Brace?" she hears from inside.

"Mr. Brace? No, it's Lady Marry."

"Oh," Nana says, cracking the door. "You, uh . . . have the same knock as him. You're dripping with perspiration, Lady Marry. What's going on?"

"I have a little problem on my hands. I shared my bed with a certain Camel, and—"

Nana is revolted. "You're into that? I mean, it's one thing to have a puppy in there with you, but . . ."

"Calm down, Nana. Not an *actual* camel. The Arab. The handsome one, who smells like fresh hummus. Or *smelled* like it, that is. I'm afraid he's . . ."

"Dead?" Nana asks.

"No, it's worse—it's—he . . ."

"Spit it out, Milady," pleads the young maid. "I've got to get up in two hours to fluff and fold the newspapers."

"What do you know about cleaning soiled bedsheets?"

Nana tries to hide her shock. "Don't tell me—"

"—I'm afraid it's true," says the humiliated Lady Marry. "Camel has wet my bed."

Nana gasps.

"That's right," says Marry. "He pissed it. Soaked it. Soiled the sheets. Took a tinkle. Made a yellow mess. Peed. Wee-weed. Sprayed his scent."

"Oh, Lady Marry," Nana moans. "We never should have gotten you that thesaurus for Christmas."

Nana and Lady Marry spend until dawn contemplating where to hide the dirty linens, as an attempt to wash them would undoubtedly arouse suspicion in the Abbey.

"How did you sleep, sweetheart?" Lord Crawfish asks Marry the next morning at breakfast.

"Very wet," she says. "I mean, very *well*."

TYPICAL MENU AT DOWNTRODDEN ABBEY

Prepared by Mrs. Patmimore

	GRANDSUN FAMILY	SERVANTS
Aperitif	Cognac	Dog water
Starter	Hot soup	Soup that was once hot
Salad	Watercress and walnuts	Stale croutons

Beverage	Spanish port wine	Cold soup
Main Course	Roast pheasant	Dry toast
Alternate Entrée	Boiled squab	Dry toast
Dessert	Fresh berries and clotted cream	Buttered toast
Dessert wine	Fine sherry	Dog water

IV

Faire to Middling

The faire arrives in town, and everyone at Down-trodden Abbey knows what that means: two weeks of listening to *"It's a Long Way to Tipperary"* and lots of inferior street food. Deep fried potatoes! What will they think of next?

The second footmasseur, Fodder, has been looking forward to the faire for some time. Genial and positive, Fodder gets along with very few of the serving staff for those very reasons. His interest in the faire is that it affords him an opportunity to invite Laizy, the scullery maid.

Laizy's tenure at Downtrodden began rather shakily, as she did not know what "scullery" meant, and for the first few weeks was afraid to ask. Once she settled in, she became indispensible. Who but a dim-witted teenager would want to spend twenty hours a day washing dishes?

From Laizy's diary, a typical workday:

4:30 a.m. There is nothing quite like a solid two and half hours of sleep. I am ready to face the day. I will pull on my well-worn corset, dress, and apron, and head downstairs to see if there are any dishes that need washing. If not, I will again wash the clean ones. Joy!

6:05 a.m. The time has come to wake the housemaids, see if the hall boy has arrived with the coal, and wash some more dishes. Life is splendid!

10:15 a.m. Tomaine and Fodder (who is quite a fetching lad) have brought the breakfast dishes in, and when I am finished with those, I can start on the pots and pans. Starting to get a little tired, truth be told, but spirits still high, all things considered.

2:08 p.m. Lunch is over, and guess what? Filthy dishes, pans, and crockery await my gentle touch. One question, diary—would it kill them to hire a second scullery maid?

6:50 p.m. Getting ready to serve supper. Not only do I get to make sure that goes well, I am also responsible for feeding the servants, who are chronically unhappy about every aspect of their responsibilities. I am near to ready to hoist a fireplace poker and jam it into my eye sockets.

8:25 p.m. Dinner is completed. Do you know what that means, diary? More pots and pans with caked-on and dried bits of food I will never be able to taste. Unless I just go ahead and start eating the trash. Then maybe I will die a quick death, and not have to get up tomorrow morning. Jk, jk! ☺

Before Fodder gets the opportunity to ask Laizy to accompany him to the faire, Tomaine makes his own overture.

"I have a great idea," he says one morning, as Laizy scrubs pudding remnants from a cauldron. "We can each wear something frilly—not the same colour—and spend the afternoon picking lavender, gossiping, and pampering ourselves with fragrant oils and tinctures."

"Rumours abound that you are a . . . 'man's man,' Tomaine."

"Where would anyone get that idea?" asks the perplexed footmasseur.

Meanwhile, Vile confronts Atchew in his office.

"I understand you are a lawyer," she says. "And I need your help."

"What is it?"

"There is a certain thing that I need to have . . . taken care of," Vile responds.

"You're going to have to be a little more specific, dowager countess. It's never been your style to mince words."

"Let me ask you a hypothetical question. Imagine that your family has, in its possession, a grand mansion—designed and built by the esteemed architect Inigo Schwartz, for instance—which has been handed down over several generations. What would you do if a certain legal loophole—an entail, let us say—kept that house from remaining in the family . . . unless a backwoods boob who doesn't know a salad fork from a sorbet spoon marries into the family?"

Atchew gets up from his chair and paces. "As only a woman with ice water in her ancient veins would do otherwise, I will assume that the mansion you reference is not Downtrodden Abbey, and the idiot you are talking about is not me. If I were in your position, I would do everything in my power to

Because British men dressed nicely, enjoyed musical theatre,
and slept with each other, it was assumed that they
were homosexuals.

make sure this clamhead you describe does not inherit the
estate."

Vile stands to leave. Her strategy has been validated.

"And by the way," Atchew says as she leaves. "Is all of that
cutlery *really* necessary?"

Later, in the village, Atchew runs into Lady Marry.

"Excuse me," he says.

Marry tells him to watch where he's going.

"So, your grandmother paid me a visit," he says. "Evidently a certain someone is set to inherit Downtrodden Abbey, and she's as annoyed as a clergyman's daughter in a leper colony."

Eating utensils, gardening instruments, and dental instruments were stored together and often confused.

"Why, that certain someone is you, Atchew." Lady Marry blushes. "Hey, that rhymes."

Atchew does a slow burn. "Ooh! That dried-up hag. How dare she try to stand in the way of our nuptials."

"Our nuptials?" Marry exclaims. "Atchew, you know I cannot be wedded to you until you've mastered the silverware. It breaks my heart to tell you this. Also, I'm not in the least bit attracted to you. But I'll tell you what—get the fork and spoon thing worked out, and we'll talk."

Back at Downtrodden Abbey, Tyresome makes a shocking discovery: a bottle of vinegar has gone missing from the pantry. Immediately, he suspects Mrs. Used, and heads to her bedroom to confront her.

"Mrs. Used," he says, peeking in.

"I did not take that bottle of vinegar from the pantry," she says, and then hiccups. "Pardon me."

"Interesting that you would raise the subject of the vinegar if you were uninvolved in its disappearance," says Tyresome. "Come on, 'fess up. Needed something for a late-night salad, perhaps? Or perhaps you had to clean some milking tools—did you know it could be used for that? Vinegar also removes rust from tools and spigots. Have a bee or jellyfish sting you need to attended to? Guess what soothes the pain? *Vinegar!*"

"Jeez—you're like a combination of Sherlock Holmes and a know-it-all apothecary. . . ."

Tyresome continues to pace, struggling to make sense of the situation.

"Perhaps you had the hiccups. One tablespoon of vinegar

and—poof—say goodbye to that problem. Trying to remove fruit stains from your hands? Guess what will do the trick there? You might even use it to relieve the discomfort of a yeast infection. Did you know that vinegar, when mixed with warm water and used as a douche, can actually adjust the pH balance in a lady's naughty bits?"

"You know something? You're kind of dreamy, and your vast knowledge of condiment usage doesn't hurt one bit," Mrs. Used whispers. It occurs to Tyresome that she may be a bit soused. "How would you like to play out my little butler-housekeeper fantasy?"

Tyresome is taken aback. He can only imagine what this might be, and inquires as to the details.

"First, we sweep the entire house. Then we scrub the baseboards. We divide the bathrooms, and then reunite to take down the drapes and beat them out back. If there is any time left, we dust the bookcases, then each retreat to our quarters, to sleep with the memories of a scintillating and most memorable evening."

"Mrs. Used, I am reasonably certain that you did not filch the bottle of vinegar," says Tyresome. "But it's quite evident that you are working way too hard. I mean, I've read that even Abraham Lincoln took time out from his presidential duties to pursue a hobby—hunting vampyres."

Across the hall, Nana lies in bed, fighting a miserable headcold. It is unlikely that she will be able to attend the faire. She is visited by Mr. Brace, who is thoughtful enough to bring her a tray.

"This would be even more delightful were it filled," Nana

says. "Like, with some tea, or scones, or porridge . . . hint-hint. . . ."

Mr. Brace cannot bear to tell Nana the truth—that he does not have the strength to carry anything heavier than an empty tray.

"Look, you wanted a tray. You failed to mention that there had to be anything on it."

"But what would I do with an empty tray?" Nana asks, genuinely perplexed.

"It's always something with you," says Mr. Brace.

"Mister Brace," Nana purrs. "We're quarrelling like an old married couple. It's actually quite dear."

"We are not a couple, Nana. I am a troubled, middle-aged cripple with erratic mood swings and a dark, unresolved past. You are a naïve, sexy young housemaid who happens to take an emotionally dangerous interest in troubled, middle-aged cripples with erratic mood swings and dark, unresolved pasts. I simply do not see how this could ever work."

Nana does a quick calculation. "Well, would you by any chance have an emotionally dangerous interest in naïve, sexy young housemaids?"

Show me a man who does not, thinks Mr. Brace. *Show me a man who does not.*

V

Where Has All the Flour Gone?

British tradition dictates that the village flour show follows the faire. For the flour show, bakers from all over England are invited to bring their sacks of processed wheat: bread flour, buckwheat flour, cake flour, gluten flour, pastry flour, rice flour, semolina flour. It is all on display in the bakers' efforts to win meaningless prizes.

At Downtrodden Abbey, Atchew visits Lord Crawfish in an effort to get some clarity.

"First of all, is your surname 'Grandsun' or 'Crawfish'?" asks the none-too-bright solicitor.

"I am Lord Roderick Crawfish, the Earl of Grandsun," replies Lord Crawfish.

"And would that make your middle name 'of,' then?"

Lord Crawfish sighs. "Surely you have not come all this way to clarify such minutiae. Please state your business."

"Actually," says Atchew, "You were the one who called this meeting."

Point taken, Lord Crawfish acknowledges. He tells Atchew that he is curious as to whether the entail to Downtrodden is in fact unbreakable. The irony is not lost on them that (a) the best available consultant is a lawyer who may have designs on his daughter and actually inherit the estate, and (b) that lawyer is not terribly bright.

"Atchew—"

"Gesundheit!" says his visitor.

"I wasn't finished. And that cannot be the first time you've used that one."

"Touché, old man," Atchew says. "Anyway—get on with it already."

"Marry's quite concerned about this business with the silverware. She can hardly be expected to spend the rest of her days with a man who employs a fish fork to eat his pudding. It was humiliating enough when she dated that fellow who thought 'Winston Churchill' was a cigarette brand, and that the capital of England was 'E.'"

In the drawing room, Lady Marry frets to the countess Flora, who has just found out that the visiting Arab wet her daughter's bed.

"We will never recover from this if word spreads," says Lady Flora. "I cannot think of a more dire situation. The only recourse may be for you to marry that dunderhead, Atchew."

"But he smells like onions, Mother. And his face is pastier than the underbelly of a mole rat. Though I grant he has a good head of hair, Atchew's ambition is also questionable. I fear that

Getting a woman drunk and fighting over her has always been a popular male activity.

if we wed, he will simply want to spend his nights lounging around at the village pub, watching cricket games on which he has wagered far too much money, and drinking ale."

"Unfortunately, you were born into an era of entitled, lazy men who take advantage of gender privilege and dominate ladies in ways that border on abuse. They earn twice as much money as women for doing less work, their thirst for alcohol is boundless, and their prehistoric sexual proclivities do not seem to evolve from where they were at puberty.

"Of one thing I am certain, however. This will all eventually change, although perhaps not until season four."

Mr. Brace limps into the pantry to locate a dessert wine for Lord Crawfish, and is surprised to see Tomaine, who quickly hides something behind his back.

"What are *you* doing in here?" asks Brace.

"Well, I can tell you what I am *not* doing," Tomaine says, sweating visibly. "I am *not* filching another bottle of vinegar."

"Another bottle? Interesting that you would phrase it that way—"

"Look, Gimpy," Tomaine shrieks. "I could buy and sell you at auction. I don't need you watching my every move and accusing me of stealing condiments. I've got plenty in my quarters—salt, pepper, even some catsup. So if I were you, I'd watch my step."

He looks at Brace's flaccid leg. "But, then again, you have to watch your step anyway, don't you? Heh-heh."

"You know," says Brace. "You might consider dealing with some of your sexual identity issues in a less aggressive manner."

"'Sexual identity issues'?" Tomaine lisps. "Honestly, what is about everyone at this place? Just because I like to get a little crazy in the parlour on Saturday nights, I scream when I hear what people are wearing to the Tony Awards, I read Oscar Wilde voraciously, I am vain about my hairline, and I have a set of Hummel figurines of Greek wrestlers in my boudoir, there is this positively outlandish assumption that I am not 'all man.' Must I take you from behind to prove otherwise?"

"Did you just say what I thought you did?" asks Brace.

"What? Um—no," says Tomaine as he backpedals out of the pantry.

Later, O'Grotten sneaks into Tomaine's bedroom.

"Look," she says. "I know you nicked the vinegar. I smelled it on your chips the other day. I can help you, mate."

Tomaine looks both guilty and slightly nauseated. "Please don't tell me I will have to bed you down in exchange for your favors."

"No, no," O'Grotten assures him. "Trust me, this is a victory-victory all the way. I want to finger Mr. Brace."

"That sounds repulsive. Have you considered talking therapy?"

"Not literally, you Nancy boy. If we can arrange for Brace to be blamed for the missing condiment, perhaps the scandal will run him out of Downtrodden Abbey. Again, not literally. As we know, 'running' isn't exactly his forte."

Tomaine's eyebrows arch (and he realizes, in the mirror, that they need plucking).

How do you separate the men from the boys in Greece?
With a crowbar.

"And if Brace is gone, who better to serve as Lord Craw-fish's lover—uh, butler—I mean, *valet*—than I?"

"Kind of where I was going with this whole thing," winks O'Grotten.

VI

When Chickens Fly

How best to describe Lady Supple Crawfish? One would have markedly better luck describing the sun, the moon, and the stars.

She is eighteen years old in 1913. Though stunning beyond belief (she has more than once been mistaken for Edwardian fashion model Kate Moth), she finds the aspirations of her contemporaries—procuring an engagement to a wealthy or titled landowner and supervising a waitstaff—inutterably shallow.

What position, you may ask, is her favourite? Well, in the perfect world Lady Supple—despite the fact that she is far too attractive—covets the position of Prime Minister of England.

Her fervent, "bleeding heart" political beliefs have made her a favourite amongst the staff at Downtrodden Abbey. She has taken a particular fancy to Handsom, the chauffeur, a similarly minded chap whose motorcar features bumper stickers reading, THE ARISTOCRACY SUCKS THE BIG ONE, DESTITUTE CHAUFFEURS MAKE MORE SUITABLE PARTNERS FOR INTERCOURSE, and WEALTHY BLOKES CAN, QUITE HONESTLY, EAT MY KNICKERS.

Handsom has supplied Lady Supple with multiple feminist pamphlets on the subject of women's rights, which have further opened her beautiful, ice-blue eyes to the fact that even a curvaceous, smoking-hot piece of Edwardian buttocks with soft, ruby lips like hers should not ever be viewed as an object of sexual desire.

After winning the right to walk outdoors, women
had the nerve to ask if they could vote.

Some of these pamphlets include "You Are No One's Crumpet, Dear Woman!" "Girdles are Hurdles," "Make Your Own Damned Scones, Buster," and "The Ladies' Guide to Politely but Firmly Advising Gentlemen to Go Piss Off."

Once Lady Supple has committed the contents of these readings to memory, Handsom makes her an enticing offer.

"Accompany me to the town square on Saturday," he pleads. "A corset-burning has been scheduled for midnight."

O'Grotten has made calculations that have led her to one conclusion—Lady Marry is younger, prettier, and wealthier than she is, and thus must be taken down a peg. And O'Grotten believes she knows how to accomplish this.

"Tomaine," she asks, as the two indulge in a cigarette break out behind the Abbey, "Have you noticed that there's something about Marry's boudoir? An inutterably foul smell?"

"Well, the wallpaper is rather heinous," Tomaine smirks. "I mean, *please*—lilac and chartreuse? Seriously? It's *so* 1897—"

"I am speaking literally, Tomaine," says O'Grotten. "There is a pungent aroma in Marry's bedroom, and it has been there ever since that Camel fellow visited."

O'Grotten stamps out her cigarette, making sure to step on Tomaine's foot as she does.

Rumours begin to circulate in London about Lady Marry, who has a nightmare in which she is featured daily in tabloid headlines:

The Guardian—"Marry Crawfish Reported to Be of Ill Repute"

The London Tymes—"Sources Claim Lady Marry Not at
  All Virtuous"
The Sun—"Marry Crawfish? What a Slut!"

Flora decides that if Marry is taking a pass on Atchew—
and "I wouldn't marry that guy if he were the last man on
Earth" certainly does seem like an indication of disinterest—
she will find another suitor for her eldest daughter.

She introduces Marry to Sir Antonio Stallion, the elderly
victim of a botched surgery in which his personality was inadvertently removed. As a result, he can only converse about two
things: bicycles and cherry cobbler.

"I'll tell you who makes a great bike," Sir Stallion tells Marry
on their first and only date. "Pashley. Their tyres are of a much
higher quality, and they've found a way to attach the derailleur
in such a manner that when one switches from low gear to
high, there is far less likelihood of it jumping the track, and—
Lady Marry, am I boring you?"

"What? Hmmnh—sorry, I must have dozed off. Surely you
can't still be discussing bicycles, though."

"Er, no, not at all. In fact, I was just going to suggest that
we head into the village for dessert. Fancy a cherry cobbler?"

"I suppose—"

"—Because I can tell you who makes the best in town.
Compton's is really wonderful. They crisp the top to a golden
brown, and carmelise the sugar, and they must use a mixture
of cherries. I can usually taste some Bing, but then all of a sud-
den a Lambert will hit my tongue, or a Rainier, and—Lady
Marry! Are you out cold again?"

Though Marry writes off Sir Stallion as a "typical male"—a poor listener who is obsessed with his own interests, in this case two-wheeled vehicles and fruity desserts—at dinner a few nights later, it is the unsightly Enid who takes a fancy to the geriatric dullard. She even goes so far as to consult the *Encyclopaedia Brittanica* for some arcane knowledge to impress him.

"My great-grandfather had a draisine, which you might not know was the first successful, two-wheeled, steerable, human propelled machine, commonly called a velocipede, and nicknamed the 'dandy horse.'"

"Good Lord," Stallion gasps to Enid. "Might you be the perfect woman for this liver-spotted romantic?"

"Only if your eyesight and judgement are both completely and utterly compromised," snaps Countess Vile.

"What's for dessert?" Lady Enid asks, sliding her veiny hand onto Stallion's bony knee. "I could seriously go for a cherry cobbler."

Marry may have rejected the old codger, but that does not stop her from resenting her sister's actions—this is Downtrodden Abbey, after all. Marry bursts into the kitchen and pulls Mrs. Patmimore aside.

"I implore you not to serve

Early bicycles had no seats, and were sold with ointments and salves.

cherry cobbler to Sir Stallion," says Lady Marry. "Regardless of his blatant wishes."

"Have you tasted Mrs. Patmimore's cobbler?" O'Grotten jumps in, between drags on her cigarette. "The true punishment would be to force him to eat it."

Lady Marry now wonders what course of action to take—to move towards the worn-out, flaccid bicycle-and-dessert-enthusiast Stallion, or to the etiquette-challenged, lunkheaded Atchew.

"What would Jesus do?" she asks the head gardener the next morning, who sadly informs her that, unfortunately, his co-worker Jesus Martinez was fired a week earlier.

That night, Enid composes a letter:

Dear Arabian Embassy,

It may be of interest to you that a certain Camel Hokky-puk was a guest at Downtrodden Abbey last month and soiled the sheets of the bed of my sister, Marry Crawfish.

I would greatly appreciate it if you would spread the word throughout the Middle East and inflict as much damage as possible to my sister's reputation, as she has been calling me "an ugly twat" since we were small children.

Sincerely,

Enid Crawfish

Lady Supple and Handsom sneak off to the village to attend a protest rally over a woman's right to attend protest rallies.

"What has got you so impassioned about this issue?" she asks him, over kettle corn, Olde Coke, and cheesesteaks.

"Me mum was an activist," Handsom explains. "She was a leading voice in the fight against influenza. Perhaps you have heard about the rally she organized in Soho Square."

"I'm terribly confused, Handsom. Isn't *everyone* against influenza? I mean, what would a protest accomplish?"

"I didn't say she was intelligent. By the way, do you know you have the most luscious lips I have ever laid eyes on?"

"No, but if you hum a few bars, I catch on pretty quick."

Back at the dear Abbey, Tyresom tells Flora that—much like like Lady Marry herself—negative stories have been circulating all across England about Lady Marry. Vile also confronts her daughter-in-law about these scurrilous tales.

"Is it true," she asks, "That there was a camel in her bed?"

"Not a camel, no," Flora assures Vile. "An Arab *named* Camel. You met him at breakfast. Remember? That sultry sultan?"

"And did the two of them have it off, then?"

"Nothing like that, Vile. He just . . . soiled her sheets."

"Honestly, Flora. How utterly unthinkable. When I was her age, such a thing never could have happened."

Of course, Flora thinks. *When Vile was Marry's age, people were still sleeping in caves.*

The business of the stolen vinegar becomes a cause célèbre at Downtrodden, with Laizy confiding to Tomaine and O'Grotten that she would do anything to protect them. Meanwhile, Mr. Brace confides to Nana that even though he's quite sure that Tomaine filched the vinegar, he would rather be accused than cost the footmasseuse his job.

"Why, I would sooner violently murder my wife before I damaged someone's ability to earn a living," says Brace.

"That's strange," Nana says. "Isn't that a bit backwards, from an ethical point of view?"

"I don't see an issue," Brace shrugs.

"Anyway, what wife? Don't tell me you're married. . . ."

"Me, married? Where would you ever get that idea? It was just a hypothetical. You've never heard the expression, 'I would sooner violently murder my wife, if I were unhappily married'?"

"No, I haven't," says Nana.

"Oh. Well. You should get out more. It's all the rage, I tell you. People are using it to replace 'sooner or later,' and 'to make a long story short.'"

At another chaotic rally with Handsom, Supple—not the most accurate golf club in the bag—mistakenly protests women's "suffrage," thinking that it means "suffering." As a result, she is hit in the head with a flying frozen chicken and knocked unconscious. Later she must face her father, who was not privy to her plans to attend the event, and most certainly would have balked at the notion.

"Hey, Pops," Supple says at dinner. "Like, what's the haps?"

"Supple, you look dazed," says Lord Crawfish. "And since when do you address me as 'Pops'? Oh, and you quite smell like poultry."

"Ah, that?" says Supple, thinking quickly. "I didn't tell you? I have been, um, using chicken fat on my skin lately. Really opens up the pores."

"Chicken fat, you say? I'll have to try that. My face has been quite dry in the past few decades."

Later, Lord Crawfish sticks his head into the kitchen and asks Laizy to set aside some chicken fat for him.

"Why, of course, sir."

"And will you see that it's delivered to my quarters before I retire?"

Laizy nods in compliance. "I'd just as soon poison my wife," she says. "As the expression goes."

"Never heard that one. Just out of curiosity—how much sleep do you get, Laizy?" asks Lord Crawfish, raising a concerned brow as the drudge walks into a wall.

"Oh, more than enough, Milord," says the kitchen maid. "Got me a full ninety minutes last night, I did."

In the parlour, Atchew waits for an opportune moment, approaches Lady Marry, and gets down on bended knee.

"Marry, do you know what this means?"

"If you've dropped a cufflink, you're on your own, Atchew. I'm blind as a bat—"

"Silly thing. I'd like your hand in marriage."

"I'm afraid it's an all-or-nothing deal. I mean, yes, I have lovely hands, but you should see the rest of me."

Atchew's back begins to hurt, so he stands, knowing that this is going to take awhile.

"Marry, 'wanting one's hand' is merely an expression. Of course I want you in your entirety. What, did you get brained with a frozen chicken as well?"

Marry paces, so excited she can barely speak.

"Wake up, darling. I'm not finished proposing."

"But what about my reputation, Atchew? Have you read *The Mail*? They'll not only claim that my sheets were soiled, but have me attending social events with the entire Manchester United football team, and indulging in some drinking game called 'Ale Table Tennis.'"

Marry tells Atchew that she's just anxious, and that she must discuss his proposal with her mother, who—being an American—tends to display good judgement (although she drinks far too many sugary beverages and favours foods laden with carbohydrates).

Flora explains to Marry that what she is experiencing with Atchew is what is known as a "cliffhanger."

"But mother," Marry pleads, "Isn't that a theatrical term?"

"It can be, darling," says Flora. "But we are a theatrical lot. I mean, imagine if we were all in some kind of continuing production, like a film series. All we do is wear fancy clothes and chatter about. There simply must be something that a viewer can latch onto and become invested in emotionally. The possibility of you and Atchew becoming man and wife is just perfect."

"Mother, you're frightening me," Marry says. "I know that there is a rumour that Mr. Tyresom once toiled as a screenwriter. Is it he who poisoned your mind with such terminology?"

"Actually, Marry," Flora says. "Just between you, me, and the flocking, I've been noodling around with an idea myself. May I pitch it to you?"

Marry goes to bed that evening devastated by the news that her mother, too, is secretly writing a story for the screen. Isn't she aware that screenwriters are the butt of every joke made about the fledgling picture industry?

Oh, and she needs to figure out that whole business about getting married, too.

VII

Rumblings and Grumblings

Spring arrives, indicating that "the Season" in London is over (whatever that means), and the Crawfish family returns to Downtrodden Abbey.

Flora feels some rumblings in her stomach and on several mornings she regurgitates. Mrs. Patmimore, the cook, is questioned, as usual, for her eyesight has been failing, and she tends to get ingredients confused, although her flounder ice cream has proven to be surprisingly popular.

Finally, Flora can take her indigestion no longer and visits a psychic, who presents a wooden ice cream stick and asks Lady Grandsun to urinate on it.

"What kind of foolishness is this?" Flora asks.

"Trust me," the psychic says.

Flora complies, and the stick turns blue.

"You're preggers."

Flora is bewildered. How could she be with child at her age? And isn't she just in for all sorts of conflict with Lord Crawfish? For starters, whether to raise the child British or American?

Flora's waistline spreads, as do rumours of her pregnancy. However, the fashions of the times do make the disguising of the so-called "infant bump" quite easy. In fact, there was a report just a few years earlier of a woman, Eleanor Hanbaskett, who was able to not only keep her out-of-wedlock pregnancies a secret, but to hide three children under her hoop skirt for most of their formative years. This was the inspiration for a music hall tune, "Mother's Special Hiding Place," which was popularized by Harry Nutzak:

Chester's on the left leg;
Dorothy's on the right.
Mama's feeling like her belt is getting way too tight!
She's due to have another;
Can't wait to see its face,
Then stick it with the others
In mother's special hiding place.
Mother's special hiding place,
Her special hiding place.
You can try to find her babies,
But you'll never see a trace!

Roderick is thrilled to hear the news of the impending blessed event, while Vile evidences complete and utter shock, as she believed Flora, at her age, to be "as barren as the Kalahari

Desert." Of course, the question on everyone's mind is what the gender of the child will be. God forbid the fortune-teller would tell me *that*, Flora thinks. Evidently, five shillings gets you *nothing* these days.

Atchew is unglued. Now the issue looms as to whether he is being rejected by Lady Marry because there is a potential new heir to Downtrodden, or simply because he is an absolute cretin.

Mrs. Patmimore's eyesight continues to be a problem, and the morning after she serves an apple-lamb-sardine pudding, Lord Crawfish makes an executive decision. Nana will accompany Mrs. Patmimore to the city, where—while the cook goes "under the knife"—she will track down Mr. Brace's mother and "grill" her about the mysteries surrounding her son.

"What would an attractive young woman like you want with my son?" asks Brace's mum. "This guy has more baggage than Paddington Station during rush hour."

She explains that after an embarrassing incident in the war—he tripped on his helmet—left him incapacitated, Brace turned to the bottle.

"He didn't just turn to it," Brace's mother recounts. "He drank it. And it was full. When he started, that is. Minutes

Loudmouth soup.

later, it was empty. Then he would open another and consume it as well. This created vast complications in his emotional life, his work life, and his marriage. He tried to stop, but could not. He felt powerless, held captive by the demon rum."

"So you're basically saying that he became an alcoholic," Nana suggests.

"Hey, that's my son you're talking about, missy. Who are you to judge?"

O'Grotten overhears a conversation between Flora and Roderick in which they mention "giving O'Grotten the ax," "firing O'Grotten," "handing O'Grotten the ol' pink slip," "sacking O'Grotten," and "canning O'Grotten's posterior."

She asks Tomaine how best to interpret what she has heard.

"I'm no genius," he says, "but I would say your days at Downtrodden Abbey are numbered. The writing is on the wall."

"You're right on the first count," O'Grotten acknowledges. "You're definitely no genius. I mean, who matches purple velvet trousers with a crimson wool vest? But, whatever.

"As far as my days being numbered and the writing being on the wall, I think what you are describing is commonly referred to as a 'calendar.' *Duh.*"

"Point taken. Nonetheless, have you considered going back to school? There is all sorts of financial aid available to unattractive, humourless, chain-smoking housekeepers. Nor would I rule out a rugby scholarship. A heifer with shoulders like yours could get a full ride to Oxford."

"I happen to have quite a bit of rapport with Handsom, the driver," O'Grotten snarls.

But the notion of attending university does capture O'Grotten's imagination, and she elects to enroll in a physics course at a nearby university.

O'Grotten attends a lecture explaining the history of using slippery objects as a means of sabotage, which gives her an idea for her final project.

Insisting that Countess Flora smells wonderful and delaying her need to bathe for several days, O'Grotten sneaks into Flora's bathroom and takes its measurements. She returns the next evening to install a series of small pulleys and monofilament wires, which she attaches to a lubricated banana skin she came across in Tomaine's bedroom. She then connects this apparatus to a lever on Lady Crawfish's bidet.

As Flora takes her first bath in days, she remarks to O'Grotten about the smell of banana permeating her nasal cavity.

"I can even detect it over your incessant smoking," she says.

O'Grotten shrugs. "How curious," she replies.

"You take such good care of me, O'Grotten," says Flora, offering a rare compliment to her maid as she steps out of the bath. O'Grotten hits the switch on the bidet, and the banana peel moves into place. But as Flora steps into her robe, she knocks into O'Grotten, who steps on the oily fruit skin. Her feet fly out from under her, and she lands on her buttocks.

Flora can barely applaud, her laughter is so overwhelming.

"*And* you keep me blessedly entertained. Bravo, O'Grotten! Who knew you could so expertly execute a pratfall? I may just write a part for you in the script I have in progress."

As O'Grotten pursues Workman's Compensation benefits,

The telephone originally frustrated its users, until a second unit was produced.

Tomaine is confronted by a furious Tyresom over his accelerating kleptomania.

"You know, I really don't need this right now," Tomaine whines. "In fact, I have a back-up plan. I want to be around men primarily, wear a fetching uniform, and have access to unlimited medication. I am considering joining the war effort as a nurse."

Meanwhile, telephones are installed in Downtrodden Abbey, to Countess Vile's continuing confusion.

"Explain it to me again, Roderick," she implores her son.

"It's simple, mother. You place your index finger into the holes corresponding to a series of seven digits that will route communication to a waiting recipient, who has also installed one of these devices. Once connected, you and the other party are able to conduct a conversation of any duration."

"How utterly ludicrous," Vile snorts.

Lord Crawfish sighs, shaking his head.

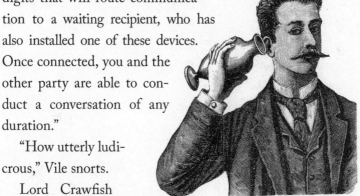

Idiot, c. 1918.

"Jesus Christ. They're setting up Call Waiting next week—but I'm not even going to bother trying to explain *that* to you."

There are rumours in the village that storylines are getting wrapped up and the family and staff flit nervously about the abbey, certain they are in the Age of Innocence, but not so sure that they are in the Age of Renewal. They have finally figured out what "the Season" is—and this could be it for Downtrodden Abbey. Therefore, all concerned are heavily invested in creating as much melodrama and gossip as possible.

Tomaine slaps Fodder on his way out. Marry makes a mess of things between Sir Stallion and Enid. Atchew tells Marry that he is sick of waiting for her to make up her mind, and he wants nothing more to do with her.

The residents seem numb and exhausted, no doubt a result of the over-the-top theatrics and physical demands of their interpersonal relationships. They are so spent that they have no reaction to a telegramme Flora reads after dinner, announcing that England is at war with Germany.

The telephone rings, which gets everyone's attention—especially Vile's.

"What is that infernal ringing?" she asks.

"Mother, please," Lord Crawfish moans. "Do we have to go through this again?"

Tyresom answers the phone. "It's for you, Wren," he says.

The diminutive housemaid scampers over and takes the receiver.

"Hello? Yes. Oh, you did, that's grand. What did you think? Uh-huh. Right. I see. Okay . . ."

"Let's get on with it, Wren," says Lord Crawfish. "You're holding up the serving of the potted grouse."

Wren puts down the receiver.

"It was my agent," she says. "I'm absolutely gobsmacked. I mean, he has some notes, but the bottom line is—he absolutely *loved* my screenplay."

Tyresom and Flora try desperately to hide their jealousy.

"This does indeed overshadow the news of war," Lady Crawfish exclaims. "But tell me—is he by any chance taking on additional clients?"

Part Two
The Second Part

VIII

Hair Apparent

W hy do they call it 'The Great War'?" Atchew asks a compatriot as they share a foxhole in the British trenches. "I mean, what's so great about sitting in a wet ditch and singing Irving Berlin songs?"

"You know something? I can see why you're having so much trouble with women," says his fellow soldier. Little does he know that Lieutenant Atchew is also hung like a gnat.

The year is 1916. At Downtrodden Abbey, the Crawfish family and their servants are also doing their part for the war effort. Fodder tries to enlist but is initially rejected for answering his recruitment interview questions in German. Roderick claims he would be willing to fight for his country, but instead forms a local organization in which members invent war stories and share them whilst imbibing huge quantities of alcohol. This, he believes, is how the aristocracy can best lend its efforts.

Weeks later, Isabich visits Downtrodden to make a star-
tling announcement: her son Atchew is returning from the
front, and will soon come back to the Abbey with his new
fiancée . . . Slovenia Swine. Enid is all too happy to break this
news to Marry, who responds by popping the inside of her
cheek with her index finger and uttering the words "Big
whoop."

"For your information, I happen to be rather taken with a
new suitor myself, Mister Dick Calamine," says Marry. "He's
quite successful in the paper business."

"Newspaper?" Enid asks.

"Not exactly. It's toilet paper, actually. With advanced
plumbing now commonplace, he smelled money, and he's absolutely cleaning up. Started his company just a few months
ago, and he's already flush. He works his ass off, and—if
things don't tank—he should be rolling in profit soon."

Meanwhile, Mr. Brace uses his yearly afternoon off to attend his mother's funeral. He is doubly sad, as it is his fervent
wish that his wife, Viral, would inhabit the grave as well. Viral
does not even have the decency to leave Brace alone with his
feelings during this difficult time. She not only attends the
ceremony, but eats well more then her fair share of cold cuts
afterwards, and attacks the dessert table with the fervour of a
rugby fullback.

Upon his return to Downtrodden, Brace proposes to Nana,
who reminds him that he is still married.

"How about this?" he suggests. "I give Viral my inheritance, and she grants me a divorce."

"Oh, great," says Nana. "So then I've not only got an old

and crippled husband, but a destitute one. I've got a better idea—you give me the inheritance, and you can stay married to Viral."

"Jeez, Nana, I was just spitballing."

"Well, I'd just as soon tell you to murder your wife than marry a penniless valet—"

"Wait—what was that? Me, murder my wife?"

"Mr. Brace, relax. It's just an expression."

Atchew arrives with Slovenia Swine. She is skinny, pale, and sickly, and no one wants to touch her or give her so much as a glance, but aside from that she is welcomed to Downtrodden Abbey. Marry pretends to like Slovenia so that she can accompany Atchew back to the train and declare her unwavering love for him.

"How can you say it is 'unwavering'?" asks Atchew. "You've changed your mind more often about me than Doozie McKay changes costumes."

"Who's Doozie McKay?"

"He's a quick-change artist. He's got a show playing in the West End. Drat! I really thought that was a clever reference."

"Look, I think we could use a break," Marry suggests.

Atchew reminds her that he is going back to fight in the war.

"Okay," she says. "That'll work. And by the way, take your time returning home."

Viral arrives at Downtrodden to let Brace know that she has no plans to grant him a divorce, and furthermore, the garage is full of his odds and ends and needs to be cleaned out. She threatens to wait Brace out if he is not compliant.

"I can't believe this. You're actually going to compromise the future legal possession of Downtrodden Abbey over a dirty garage in South London?"

"It's the principle."

"Would you be willing to grant me the divorce if I clean the garage?" Brace asks.

Mrs. Used overhears this conversation by crawling into an convenient air vent, and Tyresom watches her overhear it through a secret peephole, as Lord Crawfish happens by and sees Tyresom doing so. Lord Crawfish demands an explanation, and is especially annoyed that with everyone listening in on and spying on one another, the laundry just isn't getting done.

"You do realise that I've been wearing the same hole-ridden left sock for three days," he scoffs.

"Darn it!" groans Tyresom, embarrassed by his lack of attention to detail.

"Good suggestion," Lord Crawfish admits. "Unfortunately, I cannot sew a stitch."

Lady Supple decides that she would like to join the war effort as a nurse, in hopes of helping sponge-bathe injured soldiers and other servicemen. Though bitterly disappointed that Supple is willing to throw the best years of her life away on such nonsense, Flora sends her off with her blessing.

In a trench in northern France, Atchew runs into Tomaine, who had enlisted as a nurse as well, but secretly harboured hopes of working as an entertainer. He complains endlessly that wind, rain, and shrapnel is playing havoc with his hair, and asks Atchew to help him with it. But as he works to style Tomaine's

That's gotta *hurt.*

mane, Atchew is shot and wounded. Tomaine panics. He is scheduled to perform for the soldiers in less than an hour and his hair "will just not sit down."

The year is 1917. Prime Minister H. H. Asskiche resigns his position following a scandal in which he sent drawings of himself in the nude to an intern. He is replaced by Lloyd George David George Lloyd.

Meanwhile, in the Abbey, Lord Crawfish must deal with the consequences of Brace's exit. His new valet, Clang, is a war veteran who has survived not just the bites of giant trench rats, but attacks of poison gas, chlorine gas, phosgene gas, and mustard gas.

Rumours abound that Clang is also suffering from a little gas problem of his own, as well as consequences of the inhalation of toxins, in addition to shellshock. All of this is evidenced by the complete butchering of his duties. In particular, the regular raising of Lord Crawfish's window sash seems to be an issue, and once or twice Clang's master finds the servant actually *wearing* the sash, in the absence of trousers.

"Are you all right, Clang?" Lord Crawfish asks one evening, in a candid moment. "I'm a little concerned, as you are to assist me in shaving tomorrow morning."

"*Flammenwerfer! Flammenwerfers!*" Clang yells.

"I beg your pardon?" scoffs Lord Crawfish, his temperature rising. "There are no flamethrowers here, I assure you. Nor are there any Germans. Nor German flamethrowers. I do believe you may be suffering from some kind of post-battle trauma."

"It would be my pleasure, Milord, to assist your shaving in the morning. Once I get rid of these goddamned Krauts!"

Lord Crawfish's nerves are hardly calmed. "And by the way," he tells Clang, "For the third time, I am instructing you to *fold* the trousers and *polish* the shoes. Not the other way around."

Tomaine returns from the front line, distraught over his

Men spent weeks waxing their mustaches, often missing the event they were scheduled to attend.

split ends and the general distress of his coiffure. O'Grotten smokes two cigarettes simultaneously as she listens. But her curiosity gets the best of her.

"I've heard tell of the effects of battle—everything from psychological blindness to facial twitches, uncontrollable night sweats, diarrhoea, tremors, and the inability to eat or sleep. Not to mention anal leakage, itching and swelling, dry mouth, rashes, severe constipation, herpes, and erections lasting more than four hours. But now you're telling me—"

"—I'm telling you that I had *fantastic* hair before I shipped out. It had shine, manageability, and body. I've been brushing it continuously since my return. It's hopeless, I tell you. I'm a broken man, O'Grotten."

Isabich hears of Tomaine's troubles, and it seems to dovetail perfectly with her plan to turn Downtrodden into a hair treatment centre and salon. Vile continues to object vehemently, but shampoos and conditioners are ordered, and chairs and dryers, fueled by coal, are installed.

"Let's give Isabich a chance," Roderick tells his mother. "The importance of clean, healthy hair during wartime cannot be overestimated."

IX

About Smutt

Somehow, Atchew receives a promotion, which will take him back to England earlier than planned. Upon hearing this, Lady Marry summons Dick Calamine back to the great house in an effort to stir jealousy in Atchew.

Frustrated with Clang's work as an interim valet for Lord Crawfish, Tyresom moves him into the position of footmasseur, where he proceeds to further gum up the works. When Clang mistakes Lady Crawfish for an intruder, pins her down, and repeatedly calls her a "no good Kraut," Tyresom takes to his bed, claiming that the ensuing havoc has activated his angina.

Meanwhile, Marry grows closer to Slovenia Swine, and becomes intrigued by her irrational, inexplicable affection for Atchew.

Calamine, motivated by hostility, desperation, and greed,

*Proposals of marriage often led to
stress-induced hallucinations.*

proposes to Lady Marry, claiming that they would form a powerful aristocratic alliance. Marry meets with Nana secretly in the drawing room late at night, confiding in her and desperate for advice.

"What do you see in Brace?" she asks. "I mean, on paper it's a complete mismatch—a young, naïve waif and a middle-aged, married, been-through-the-mill personal valet."

"I like it," says Nana, thinking.

"What do you mean, you like it?" asks Marry.

"Well, it's a meet cute. I've been looking for something I could develop as a story for—"

Marry moans. "Please don't say what I think you're going to."

Nana confesses that she, too, has been working on a screenplay, but a dearth of marketable ideas has stopped her cold.

"I tried the whole 'fish out of water' thing, with a character based on Clang—you know, the dunderheaded valet. But it just seemed like a series of unconnected incidents.

"Then there's the sad story of Tomaine, and his latent sexual identity issues. Wasn't sure that would sell. I mean, does anyone actually *read* Gertrude Stein, or does everyone just buy the book and sit around in cafés pretending to care whether she's getting it from a bloke or a lass?

"I noodled around a little with Lady Crawfish's pregnancy, and the entail, and how one affected the other, and the this whole thing with you and Atchew, and that Calamine fellow. . . ."

How dare she turn my family's life into fodder for a gossipy melodrama, Marry thinks. But against her better judgement and despite this accelerating ire, Lady Marry finds herself becoming curious.

"And where did that go?"

Nana shrugs. "It just felt more like a theatrical drama, not a full cinematic experience—"

"I am appalled. Firstly, that you have joined the ranks of what appears to be half the inhabitants of this house—delusional screenwriters. And secondly, that you have reduced the goings-on at Downtrodden Abbey to the level of insipid entertainment of the type one would find broadcast on the radio as a source of prurient popular entertainment."

"What's a 'radio'?" asks Countess Vile, overhearing the conversation.

Lady Marry explains to her grandmother the intricate matrix of vacuum tubes, wiring, and electronic signals that mesh to form radio, one of the more important advances in communication of the nineteenth century.

"Sounds like a lot of poppycock to me," Vile snorts. "Next you'll be telling me that a system of receptors in the sky can beam down driving directions for motorcars, both visually and spoken, on small screens in the vehicles themselves."

Marry listens to Vile gas on for several minutes prior to suggesting that such wild thoughts are undoubtedly the product of sleep deprivation. When the dowager countess leaves the drawing room, Marry shakes her head sadly.

"Honestly, that woman is madder than a snake," she says.

"There is something wonderful about her imagination," says Nana. "I mean, that whole thing about the interconnected system of receptors—I must give her credit—that is really inventive."

A passel of returning soldiers file into Downtrodden Abbey, whose rooms are converted into stations to shampoo, rinse, cut, and blow-dry the men's hair before determinations are made regarding the larger issues of scalp treatment, hairpieces, and surgical follical replacement.

Under Isabich's direction, Tomaine takes over as a consultant, conducting intakes on each of the officers and diagnosing his individual styling needs.

Handsom takes a walk with Supple, and reveals his plans to claim his right to refuse to perform military service as a conscientious objector.

"Have you got a strategy?" Supple asks.

"I'm thinking of fleeing up to Scotland," Handsom says. "Did you know they don't pay for health insurance there? And everyone has guns, but no one uses them?"

On furlough, Atchew visits Downtrodden in the middle of one of Tomaine's hissy fits, but is still impressed with the high level of hair care being offered. Marry, meanwhile, discovers through Dick Calamine that Brace did not actually return to his house in South London—he has been spotted daily in a village tearoom, where word has it that he sits for hours on end with a notebook and fountain pen.

Marry shares this information with Nana, who travels to the village on her day off, scouring each and every tearoom for her beloved. Finally, she locates Brace, who is scribbling away feverishly.

"Brace—Brace, it's I," says Nana.

"Hang on a second," he responds, making another entry in his book.

"Brace, what are you doing? I was under the impression that you were cleaning your garage, and now I hear that you're spending your days sitting in this tearoom."

Brace realizes that this is an opportunity to be completely honest, as Nana is the one woman with whom he feels emotionally safe.

"Promise me you won't tell anyone," he pleads, his eyes welling with tears.

"I promise," Nana says.

"No, seriously—pinkie swear."

Nana rolls her pale blue eyes. "Come on, Brace, I only

have a few hours off. I'm supposed to go muck out the horse stalls."

"That's as a good a segue as any, I suppose," says Mr. Brace. "I'm actually working on a—"

"—Oh, God, not another—"

"It's a novel," Brace explains. "A big, sprawling epic set in an estate in England, concerning a group of downstairs servants and the upstairs family they work for. Oops, ended that sentence with a preposition. Trust me, I'm a better writer than that, heh-heh. Anyway, it's from the point of view of a valet who's handsome, hobbled, and haunted."

"Is it autobiographical?"

"Why would you say that?"

Nana wipes her brow. "I'm just relieved that you're not working on a screenplay," she says. "I mean, it's like bubonic plague—everyone I talk to thinks they have a good idea for a motion picture. Crikey, when I started working on mine, there was very little competition. But coupled with the transformation of Downtrodden Abbey into some kind of palatial beauty parlour for war veterans, I just feel like we're losing our identity."

Handsom is turned down for military service due to overly audible snoring.

Meanwhile, Enid flirts incessantly with the incoming visitors to the hair treatment center, washing, deep-conditioning, and rinsing, and experiencing the satisfaction of being of service. Vile returns from a visit with Slovenia in London as the Crawfish family is dining.

"Are you sitting down?" she asks.

"Of course," says Lord Crawfish. "What does it look like?"

"It's an expression. I have a juicy piece of gossip. It seems that Atchew's fiancée, Slovenia, is a spy. She stole documents from her uncle's cousin's friend's brother's sister-in-law, which were then given to Dick Calamine . . . who she is sleeping with, by the way."

Lady Marry is devastated. She is torn between a philistine who cannot differentiate his eating utensils and a lecherous toilet tissue magnate. As it happens, they are each carrying on with another woman, who happens to also be the same woman. Her mind thoroughly boggled, Marry takes to bed for several days, with a stack of magazines and a frozen cheesecake she finds in the icebox, made in town by a certain Miss Tess Coe.

Laizy expresses concern that when Fodder returns from the front lines, he will not only continue to pursue her, but ask her complicated math problems, one of his many irritating habits. Mrs. Patmimore assures Laizy that Fodder is a buffoon who will accept love from just about anything. She suggests that Laizy try to encourage a romance between Fodder and a Persian rug in the library.

General Smutt, a decorated officer, visits Downtrodden Abbey for dinner. Tomaine proceeds to *re*decorate him. While a brilliant military strategist, Smutt is known to possess a filthy mind, with no filter between his prurient thoughts and his tongue.

"A mighty tasty piece of meat," Smutt says as he chews Mrs. Patmimore's leathery prime rib while eyeing Lady Supple. "In fact, I could see sharing the rest of my life with it and making it do all sorts of nasty things to me in the bedroom."

"Happy to see that our cook hasn't lost her touch," says Lord Crawfish, never one to comprehend double entendre.

"General, why don't you keep *your* meat in your trousers?" Supple suggests.

"I would be happy to tenderize the general's meat," offers Enid.

"Keep your day job, Tootsie," General Smutt says. "Has anyone ever told you that you've got a face for radio?"

"Why is everyone so consumed with this blasted 'radio' gizmo?" asks Vile, shaking her jowls huffily.

In the pantry, Nana finds a note written by Handsom, saying that by the time she reads this, he will be getting carted off to jail for pulling the general's chair out from under him when he moves into the drawing room after dinner.

At the last minute, however, as he approaches the chair in question, Handsom is wrestled to the ground by staff members, as is the chair. Handsom tells Supple that he was only planning to embarrass the general, and he had a rubber chicken and a whoopee cushion at the ready if the chair stunt had failed. As amusing as those pranks may have been, he awaits rather serious consequences for his actions.

Fodder proposes to Laizy. Rather than hurt his feelings she decides to accept, and spend the rest of her life in the company of the dim-witted social outcast.

As for Clang, Lord Crawfish must take him aside and deliver some harsh news.

"Clang, I'm afraid I'm going to have to let you go."

"Go where?"

Lord Crawfish sighs. He knew this was going to be difficult.

"Your services are no longer required at Downtrodden Abbey."

Clang beams. "Oh, that's smashing—you mean I can just live here now and have everyone else do the labourious bits?"

Much as the sounds of dishes smashing, windows breaking, and the disappointment over his inferior domestic skills will be missed, Lord Crawfish walks Clang to the front door, hands him a five pound note, and kicks him down the steps.

MEALTIMES FOR THE STAFF

Breakfast, dinner, and supper constitute the basic servant meals, as opposed to the seven meals partaken by the family.

Beer is the only staple in the servants' diet. A beer allowance is provided for those who do not wish to drink beer at mealtime. There has never been one beer redeemed for cash in the history of Downtrodden Abbey.

Servants serving servants can be a challenging business. Seating is based on the hierarchy of the staff. The head butler sits at the head of the table. The lowliest, most junior maid will sit *under* the table. Male servants sit on one side, and females along the other. Games

Early corkscrew, c. 1908.

of "footsie" are strictly forbidden, but this activity is difficult to police and goes on nonetheless.

At dinner the butler carves the meat, then has his work inspected by the footmasseur, who writes a detailed report and hands it to the valet. If the valet's approval is met, the platter is given to the housekeeper, who serves the vegetables and arranges the garnish. Once the scullery maid approves the arrangement of the vegetables and garnish on the plate, the plates are distributed for consumption. By this this time, however, often the allotted time for the servants to eat has expired.

Pretty depressing, huh?

X

Sunday Roast

Enid has one of her brilliant ideas—to stage a roast in order to lift the spirits of the soldiers who have not quite yet figured out what to do with their hair.

The much-anticipated event is reviewed by the *London Tymes*, in a snippy tone that makes many suspect that the writer is none other than Tomaine:

> *Downtrodden Abbey served up a Sunday roast last night, but it was hardly a nourishing one.*
>
> *Roastmaster General for the evening was Lord Roderick Crawfish, the Earl of Grandsun—hardly an inspired choice for a comedy show, if you have ever met the bloke—who welcomed the assembled in the estate's Great Hall.*
>
> *"It's splendid to have everyone here at Downtrodden*

Abbey," Lord Crawfish began. "You know, this place is so vast that Countess Flora and I each sleep in separate counties."

The roast's attendees, particularly the servants, were hardly amused by this alleged jest, which only pointed out the financial inequity and the class warfare many have predicted will eventually destroy England. Noses were thumbed en masse by the embittered Downtrodden staff, whom the earl nonetheless targeted for his next sorry attempt at wit.

"Seriously, though, I'm so glad the servants have elected to attend tonight," Lord Crawfish continued, as he perspired and tugged at his bowtie nervously. "Now, I don't want to say most of you are quite poor, but I don't think the lot of you could even afford to pay attention."

"Why should we? You stink!" one of the maids shouted from the back, as an overripe tomato whizzed by Lord Crawfish's head.

"You're fired!" said Crawfish, earning his first (and last) laugh of the evening.

"Our first speaker is Lady Enid," Crawfish introduced his unattractive middle daughter. "I am not saying that Enid is homely, but when she was born, the countess said to me, 'What a treasure!' and I replied, 'You're absolutely right! Let's bury it!'"

Lady Enid, heiress to her father's lack of timing and clearly unaware of what constitutes a roast—or entertainment, for that matter—followed with an impassioned but dreadfully boring description of the Abbey's transformation into what she believes is "a destination for soldiers with *challenging coiffure issues. A haven for fallen warriors with rising hairlines, one might say." A derby was passed, and donations accepted.*

Next up was Isabich Crawfish, who trotted out her semi-popular "You're so old" jokes with the guest of honour, as usual, serving as her foil. Isabich (no spring chicken herself) managed to land a few zingers at the ancient dowager countess's expense.

Finally, it was time for Vile to take the stage. She opened by thanking her son for hosting.

"This is the most strenuous activity Roderick has engaged in for quite some time," said Vile. "I mean, seriously—this guy is so lazy, he sticks his nose out the window so that the wind can blow it for him!"

The crowd—particularly the servants, in this instance—roared.

"Raising Roderick taught me something very important. Give a man a fish and he will eat for a day. Teach him how to fish, and he will still merely sit on his useless rump all day and have others prepare the fish for him."

All in all, it was a night to remember—remember not to attend next year, that is.

Flora reaches the end of her rope regarding the use of Downtrodden Abbey as a hair care centre, and confronts Isabich.

"This is absurd," Lady Crawfish snaps. "I'm sick and tired of walking the halls and smelling mousse, pomade, shampoo, and hair spray. "And has there been any improvement? These men aren't looking any better. I see parts on the wrong side. I see uneven sideburns, and ill-advised mustaches. Face it, Isabich—this was a lousy idea. I mean, why not open a big and tall men's shop in Tokyo while you're at it?" *Damn*, she thinks. *That line would have killed at the roast.*

"I have had quite enough of your incessant criticism, Flora," counters Isabich. "I am seriously considering moving to France, the true home of the pompadour and coiffure—where hair styling is honoured and revered."

In the parlour, Vile has tea with Marry, with the express purpose of querying her about Supple's taste in men.

"There is something seriously wrong with your sister," says Vile. "I've never known her to take a special interest in gardening, yet she will talk for hours on end with a lowly groundskeeper. Her fascination with mechanics has also been a well-kept secret—how else could one explain the endless conversations she conducts in the garage with that driver—?"

"Handsom?"

"He's all right, I suppose. I tend to go for the swarthy, ruggedly intelligent countenances of Louis Pasteur or Alfred Nobel—"

"That's his *name*, is what I meant," says Marry. "The chauffeur. Handsom."

"And would you surmise that Supple has designs to permanently join souls with this lowly, destitute, poor-as-a-churchmouse, bread-sandwich-eating motorcar jockey? I mean no judgement, of course—I am merely curious."

Meanwhile, Lord Crawfish receives a letter from Calamine:

My Dear Lord Crawfish:

It has come to my attention that asking for your daughter Marry's hand in marriage without first speaking to you was a frightful breach of etiquette. I implore you to understand that this lack of judgement is in no way indicative of my character. It was not my intent to insult someone as insecure, sensitive, intolerant, and egocentric as you. Please accept my apologies, although I fear you may not, because my experience of you is that you tend to be pigheaded and rigid.

Under separate cover, I am sending a fruit basket, in hopes that the sweet flavour of produce will diminish the sour taste in your mouth from this unfortunate event. I would continue to apply euphemism and evocative metaphor to this situation, but I have used up my quota on an earlier letter in the service of battling a violation for urinating in public.

Respectfully,
Dick Calamine

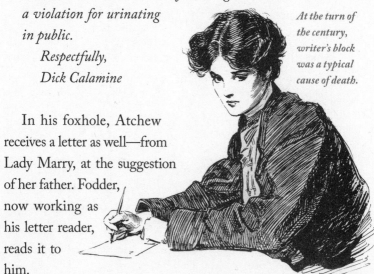

At the turn of the century, writer's block was a typical cause of death.

In his foxhole, Atchew receives a letter as well—from Lady Marry, at the suggestion of her father. Fodder, now working as his letter reader, reads it to him.

Dear Atchew:

So, how's it going? Is your foxhole comfortable? Have you been shot? That would be horrible. I mean, if anything were to happen to you, I would just be devastated. Really. You must believe me. Just thinking about it upsets me to no end. It would be difficult for me to go on. I'm quite literally shaking as I write this.

Anyway—enough small talk. I have a bit of news that may get your knickers in a twist. (By the way, do they allow you to wear knickers there? Just curious.)

Turns out I fancy Dick quite a bit. I'm not sure if I can live without Dick. I've got a real thing for Dick. Not Spotted Dick—the British food that makes every tourist laugh when they hear of it—but Dick Calamine. You know. That older, manipulative, divisive plutocrat and social climber? Well, if you've got daddy issues like I do, a man like Calamine is irresistible.

I sincerely hope I haven't ruined your day.

Warmly,

Marry

Word spreads around Downtrodden that Mr. Brace now spends his days in a local pub, a writing tablet on his laptop, hard at work on a novel. Feeling badly about the manner in which Brace was dismissed, Roderick ventures into town to visit his hobbled friend.

"I can't talk about it—if I talk about it, I won't write it," Brace says, over a pint with Lord Crawfish.

"Oh, I understand. I'm not here to talk about your novel, though. It's . . . Atchew."

"Gesundheit."

"No, Brace. Atchew—Marry's intended. He was to return from war, and no one's heard from him. Everything's all out of kilter. There's constant gossip and backstabbing, and every conversation is overheard and repeated to some inappropriate party."

"Sounds quite a bit like business as usual, Milord."

Roderick's eyes well with tears. "Would you consider returning to Downtrodden?" he asks. "It's only a quarter of a kilometer away. If you start now, you'll be there by Christmas."

Brace recaps his activities over the past few weeks, as he worked to find a valid reason to leave his marriage to Viral. He felt he needed a more substantial argument in court than hers (that Brace refused to clean the garage).

He first suspected wrongdoing when he saw a razor and shaving soap. Then, several pairs of men's trousers, suspenders, and neckties in the closet. "These were all hints that something was awry," Brace told Lord Crawfish.

"I should say so."

"Initially, it seemed obvious—she was dressing in men's clothing and shaving her face! Then I discovered a stack of love letters—not written by me—on perfumed stationary, in the drawer of Viral's nightstand.

"So it's a full-on split personality, I thought. In the guise of this male character, Viral is writing poetry to herself. But that's hardly grounds for divorce."

Lord Crawfish does his best not to offend his dear colleague.

"Brace, you jackass! Men's clothing? Foreign shaving equipment? Love letters? Use your bean, old man. She's cuckolding you. Catting around. Cheating."

Brace is gobsmacked. He cannot imagine why his wife would want to play around on a war-ravaged cripple who is in love with a sleep-deprived maid.

"I think it is time for me to take you up on your offer to return to Downtrodden Abbey, Lord Crawfish," he says. "It is simply the right atmosphere for someone as emotionally fragile and sensitive as I am.

"But first, I'm going to put a cap in that bitch."

The war rages on, as Atchew and Fodder toil for the Fourth Army. Following the discovery of a typographical error, the Offensive Hundred Days is changed to the far more threatening-sounding Hundred Days Offensive. As the Allied Forces advance, though, Fodder notices Atchew choking on a piece of food.

Fodder has heard talk that the Germans have been developing a secret method of forcing lodged particles from one another's throats, but that is hardly helpful now.

Fortunately, he has been carrying a cannonball, a lucky charm from his great-grandfather. This confused Fodder at the time of the gift and has greatly compromised his mobility, but he is grateful to have the cannonball at this moment. With a running start, he thrusts the cannonball into the suffering Atchew's stomach. From Atchew's mouth a bullet shoots out, with such force that it severely disfigures Fodder.

Atchew is transported back to Downtrodden Abbey with Fodder, who is now unrecognizable and initially sent away, as he is thought to be an anonymous solicitor selling magazine subscriptions door-to-door. As Atchew is still stricken with laryngitis from the bullet in his throat (which he later claims he mistook for a ration of chewing gum), he cannot remedy the situation.

Oddly enough, it is the intolerant and thick-headed Vile who convinces the others that the unwanted stranger is Fodder, and that he should convalesce within the hallowed walls of Downtrodden Abbey. With some trepidation, she pitches the notion to Isabich.

"I refuse to compromise my ideals for some frivolous, impulsive fantasy," Isabich tells the dowager countess.

"Seriously? You don't think the recuperation of a badly injured soldier is more important than the cosmetic needs of a bunch of pansies?"

"I will thank you not to insult my clients," Isabich counters. "Here's a compromise. We'll do an initial consultation with Fodder and try to fit him in. Paolo is completely booked, but Franco might be able to see him if it's just a cut, and he's not too concerned about the color."

Meanwhile, Marry is reunited with Atchew, who slowly begins to recover his voice, but after several meetings in close quarters must admit to a chronic case of irritable bowel syndrome.

"It's said that war does funny things to men," he chokes out. "But what they do to the food is anything but amusing.

You should have seen this stuff they foist on officers, Marry. Bruised produce. Lumpy porridge. Wine of unacceptable vintages. I dropped a biscuit on my foot and fractured three toes."

"Good God," gasps Lady Marry. "No wonder you were chomping on bullets. Not that I would turn to artillery as a source of nutrition or flavour but—as they say—different strokes."

"No one seems to understand that the bullet episode was unintentional. What is it with you people? One would think *you* were the ones who had suffered brain trauma."

When Slovenia Swine arrives at Downtrodden Abbey, she and Atchew take a long walk around the grounds. But even amongst the roses, she cannot help but notice a certain un-pleasant aroma trailing her intended.

"You look good, Atchew," she says. "I wish I could say the same about the way you smell."

Atchew knows that he cannot ignore the elephant odor in the room.

"Slovenia," he says, taking her hand, "What would you say if I told you that I might never be able to . . . make a normal movement again?"

"Your movements look fine," she says reassuringly. "I mean, I've heard reports of soldiers returning with spinal injuries, needing wheelchairs, and—"

"—I'm talking about *bowel* movements, my dear. Chronic flatulence. Diarrhoea. Loose stool. Darling, you can do much better than me. You owe it to yourself, for a better life—a life

"Pull your finger? For heaven's sake, why?"

in which you don't have to leave a room every time your husband enters it. A life in which my special dietary needs do not take precedent over those of our own children.

"Rather than continuing to think that you *smell* something that is dead, I urge you to consider *me* dead."

Brace puts his novel writing on hold to return to Downtrodden Abbey, but his reappearance is hardly heralded, particularly by Tomaine—who is gunning for the position as Lord Crawfish's personal valet—and O'Grotten, who feels obliged to write an encoded letter to Viral:

Dear Mrs. Brace,

You do not know me, but I have information about a cer-
tain hobbled party to your marriage who is not you. I would
rather not name names. The gentleman in question has de-
fied your wishes and returned to a certain vast manor in the
countryside, where he may or may not have been employed by
a certain lord, possibly as his valet.

Sincerely,

An Anonymous Homely, Chain-smoking Yenta and
Occasional Housekeeper

O'Grotten feels confident that Viral Brace will be able to
read between the lines. Her husband, meanwhile, literally falls
back into Nana's emaciated arms, but is ecstatic that he has
elected to carry out his plan: to give every one of his last remaining pennies to his wife in order that she will divorce him.

"Just think," he tells Nana. "Now, not only will you be with
a guy that people will mistake for your grandfather, but you'll
be broke, and have to take yourself out of the workforce in order to care for me in my dotage."

Brace's image of their future together sounds absolutely
nauseating to Nana, but she keeps this opinion to herself as he
returns to his duties at the Abbey. Brace notices her hangdog
countenance. When he asks if she would like to hear about his
aborted novel, Nana demurs, telling him that she finds it even
more excruciating than listening to people recount their
dreams.

Viral Brace arrives at the Abbey and calls for a private
meeting with Roderick and Flora Crawfish.

"I understand that an Arab wet your daughter's bed," she says.

"What concern is that of yours?" the earl asks.

"It's simple. I've devised a plan that will have serious consequences. I will go to Dick Calamine, who will insure that this humiliating incident is printed on every roll of toilet paper in England. If Calamine buys the story from me and doesn't run it on the papers, he can use it as a way to blackmail Marry. But if that happens, then I'll need a back-up plan, which may involve hiring a team of private investigators to follow Brace and catch him with this young maid he's purportedly seeing. And don't think it's easy to get these detectives to focus, what with the Christmas holidays coming. Plus, they charge a bloody fortune."

"Why, that doesn't sound simple at all," Lord Crawfish says.

"What can I say?" Viral shrugs. "It's a work in progress."

Knowing that Marry has been having second thoughts about marrying him, Calamine elects to pretend that they are already married, hoping that she will fall into step. Calamine begins arguing with Marry incessantly, sleeping on the sofa in the drawing room, and complaining about her weight gain to his male friends.

The unsightly Fodder is installed in the salon, where—unfortunately—a good hairstyle will hardly erase the horror Laizy feels when she looks at him.

"Marry me," Fodder pleads, when they have a moment alone. "Just think about it, at least. You'll have a king's ransom—my military pension—if I die, which could be any minute now . . ."

"There's a better chance that I'll be the one who dies—of humiliation," Laizy moans. "Honestly, Fodder. I can't tell your face from your rear end. What kind of a life could we possibly have together?"

"Look me in the eye and say that," Fodder challenges.

"I'd have better luck milking a rooster. Who even knows where your eye is?" asks Laizy. "But I'll consider your offer. I mean, not that scrubbing pots and dishes and mopping the floors all day and night isn't a good life. I would like a formal, printed statement with the exact amount that I would inherit, however."

"Honestly, Laizy, you must be the most romantic gal I have ever known."

"That's great, Fodder," Laizy says, as she adjusts his bed-clothes and tiptoes out of his bedroom. "You just make sure to stay on your medication, okay?"

Handsom starts to read more and more about the work of Georgi Plekhanov, who believed that Russia—less developed in industry than Western Europe, would need to replace tsarism with a socialist, and eventually a communist, society.

"You seem so serious lately," Lady Supple tells Handsom during a walk through the woods.

"Listen. Karl Marx thought that Russia might avoid a period of bourgeoisie capitalism. Something must be done. A revolution might be a harbinger—the beginning of workers' revolutions all over the Western world."

"I'm concerned that you may be verging on political zealotry," says Supple. "I mean, we used to discuss what kind of dog we wanted, and where to get the finest scones and tea. Now you're obsessed with the murder of the tsar, and social change. To be perfectly honest it's, like, kind of a bring-down."

"What if we were to sneak behind those bushes and I took you in much the manner that Stalin plans to someday overthrow the efforts of the Trotskyites to remove him from power?" Handsom proposes.

"Now you're talking, big fella."

Atchew's recovery is slow, so he is cared for by Lady Marry—who fails to fall for Calamine's ruse, much to the bathroom tissue magnate's chagrin. Atchew can barely be heard as his damaged larynx continues to slowly heal, but he does pantomime to Marry that she should be careful not to destroy her life by marrying him. Between his war injury and his continuing confusion over cutlery, Atchew believes that Marry's domestic future lies with someone else.

Calamine still believes he is the man for Marry to marry, and in that spirit he considers making an impulsive purchase—a grand estate located a mere stone's throw from Downtrodden Abbey. He responds to the following advert in the local newspaper:

HOARE HOUSE

Forty-one bedroom, thirty-six bath manor. Architect Nathan Trevathon's masterpiece. Hardwood floors. Sixty-seven acres. Private lake. Golf course. Kitchen recently redone. Great location. Stunning views. Garage fits two carriages or three motorcars. Rustic barn perfect for rental or romantic trysts. Finished deck.

Demure woman and lecherous creep, c. 1914.

French doors. Comfortable parlour. Study ideal for studying. Wine cellar. Media room equipped with fully functional telegraph. Owner is former king, highly motivated to sell. Offered at £100,000,000. Serious inquiries only. Perfect for businessman trying to finagle his way into family entail. No barons, please.

XI

Stupid Pettrick

A request comes in to Downtrodden from a young man, Pettrick Thunderbird, asking for a haircut and style. Enid takes a particular fancy to him, and after they spend some time together, she suspects him to be Lady Marry's intended, who was thought to have perished on the *Gigantic*.

No one seems to recognize the fellow. As there were no photographs of Pettrick, and—as seems to happen with most men who stray too far from the Abbey—he was disfigured, the Crawfish family decides to ask him a series of questions over dinner.

"Say, what can you tell us about the *Gigantic*, if you were really on it?" the suspicious Lord Crawfish begins.

"Well, the ship was eight hundred and eighty-two feet, nine inches long, with a maximum width of ninety-two feet, six inches. Her height from keel to bridge was one hundred and four feet. She weighed forty-six thousand, three hundred and twenty-eight tons. There were ten decks, eight of which were for passenger use. They were called The Bridge, The Promenade, the Saloon Deck, the Upper Deck, the Middle Deck, the Lower Deck, and the Shelter Deck—"

"I'm beginning to think he wasn't just a passenger on the boat," snorts Vile, the dowager countess. "He may have built the blasted thing."

Enid starts to ask Pettrick how he knew the ship's gender, and is immediately silenced by the others.

"All right, all right. So you know a lot about the ship. What's with the surname—'Thunderbird'?" the earl asks. "Your given name was 'Crawfish.'"

"I must have gotten this other name off of a wine bottle or something. I banged my head on the hull of the *Gigantic* and my memory has been unreliable ever since. Who are you people, anyway? And what am I doing here? And would you like to hear the dimensions of the *Gigantic* some time? I banged my head on its hull, and my memory has been unreliable ever since."

"Please God, no," groans Vile.

Lady Marry sits in silent prayer, hoping against hope that this idiot does not remember that she was to be his bride.

Later, in a private moment with her father, Marry insists that the man claiming to be Pettrick is a fraud, and encourages him to consult Miss Marple to investigate. When Lord Crawfish informs his daughter that Marple is a fictional character, she is stumped and takes to bed. When she awakens, Atchew is gone, certain that between Pettrick whoever-he-is and Calamine, Marry's dance card is full.

Meanwhile, Calamine starts making plans to share Hoare House not just with one roommate, but two. He asks Tyresom to consider moving over to work as his and Lady Marry's butler.

"I would never and could never be in the employ of anyone but Lord and Lady Crawfish," Tyresom responds. "He is the kindest, most loyal master I have ever served, and I've become quite attached to him over the years. She is equally lovely and feels like a sister to me. It is simply out of the question."

"That's a shame," says Calamine. "I was planning to pay you another ten shillings a week."

"You know what?" counters Tyresom. "Let me think about it. Sometimes change is a good thing."

Roderick can barely stand the machinations that seem to have taken over Downtrodden Abbey. Calamine summons Slovenia to seduce Atchew in the likely event of his return, to lure him away from Lady Marry. Flora supports this devious plan, fearful that the product of an Atchew-Marry union would be a child who also cannot choose the right fork with which to eat an entrée.

Lord Crawfish's only solace is the appearance of a new maid at the great house.

She arrives on a crisp autumn breeze and virtually melts Roderick's heart on sight, sweeping him off his feet like a mixed metaphor that wants to be a simile but ends up one big confusing cliché.

Her name is Jen Nehsayqua, and she definitely has a certain something. But it is not the woman who catches Lord Crawfish's fancy—it is her eight-year-old son, Fergie. In Fergie, he seems to see possibility. Is he the son Roderick never had? The very heir to Downtrodden Abbey, in short knickers and a beanie? Does the Earl of Grandsun look at this pre-pubescent lad and, quite possibly . . . see himself?

"Roderick, you bloody ninny," Flora says in their bedroom, on the evening of the mother and son's appearance. "You're looking in the mirror."

Realizing he must keep his growing obsession covert, Lord Crawfish attempts—with varying degrees of success—to hide his interest in the boy.

Mr. Brace receives news that Viral—refusing to grant him a divorce—has presented the judge with a roll of tape with which she claims he bound her one evening after a fierce argument over fornication. He is particularly dismayed to see how the tabloid papers are handling the matter:

SEX TAPE SCANDAL

The crippled valet of one of England's most prosperous men, Roderick Crawfish, the Earl of Grandsun, is apparently the focus of an inquiry brought on by his disgruntled wife. Court papers reveal that in November, John Brace reportedly used tape to fasten his wife Viral to a banister and read her the complete works of Geoffrey Chaucer. His attorney has a sore throat and is unable to comment. The London Library claims that the Chaucer books have been overdue for several weeks, and Brace faces stiff penalties.

"This is an outrage," Brace complains to Lord Crawfish. "I don't even like Chaucer."

"Seriously? You can't mean that. He's the father of English literature, dear boy. He put Middle English on the map, at a time when French and Latin were the dominant languages in England."

"You're missing the point, Milord. These papers are constantly getting the facts wrong. This is a major embarrassment. I fear that Nana will leave me when she hears of the mere mention of these alleged misdeeds."

Lord Crawfish is not so sure, suspecting that Nana may simply be impressed with Brace's newfound celebrity.

"Wasn't it Gainsborough," he notes, "Who said that in the future everyone will be well-known for a quarter of an hour?"

Indeed, Nana is elated, even aroused, when she hears that her paramour has made headlines in the local press.

"I had no idea you liked Chaucer," she tells him. "And tape—how ingenious! Perhaps you can try that on me. With less nefarious intent, of course."

"Nana," Brace says. "Calm down. You cannot believe everything you read. This is merely a sign of the age we in which we are living. Someday the news media will be a reliable bastion of factual information, not a hotbed of gossip and falsification. Mark my words."

Brace impulsively heads to London to confront Viral, who is now not only famous, but is frequently compared to the Paris Hilton, due to a radical weight gain and certain boxy appearance during her last few stressful months.

At the increasingly dreary abbey, Lord Crawfish is forced to put his trousers on one leg at a time and all by himself in

Brace's absence. He misses the sound of his old friend clomping up and down the stairs for hours at a time.

Brace, meanwhile, scours the London Library for a proper guide as to how to murder his wife in a gentlemanly manner. He stumbles upon *Award-Winning Rat Poison Recipes*, which contains the following:

Strawberry-Rhubarb Rat Poison Compote

INGREDIENTS:

One pound fresh Strawberries
One pound Rhubarb
Two cups sugar
Three teaspoons industrial strength rat poison

DIRECTIONS:

Stew rhubarb in one cup of water. Add strawberries and continue heating mixture. Stir in sugar to taste. Add rat poison. Serves one unwanted spouse.

When Brace returns, he is close-mouthed to everyone but Nana. The others can only imagine what may have happened between Brace and Viral during their unscheduled reunion.

"It was a dark and stormy night," he begins, during a late-night rendezvous with his beloved scullery maid.

"Seriously?" she asks. "You call yourself a novelist, and you're starting the story with 'It was a dark and stormy night'?"

Brace shakes her by the shoulders, hoping to knock some sense into her.

"Look. For your information, the writing thing was just a lark, something to do between valet appointments. I would have thought you would want to know the truth about what everyone else is conjecturing upon. I know, I know—I ended that sentence with a preposition. But would you please just *listen*?

"I rode the midnight train to Paddington Station. In the bar car, I had a Pimm's with extra cucumber and some crisps. I sat next to an elderly woman who told me she was a fortune-teller, with clairvoyant abilities. She also did light housekeeping, and showed me how to remove a stain on my vest. Oh, and it turns out she was from Bristol, where my uncle had a fishing boat, and—"

Nana has fallen asleep. For the time being, Brace will have to keep his secret to himself.

The next evening at dinner, Lord Crawfish announces that the night's activity would be another game of charades.

Drawing the first card, Roderick reads it, then points to his arm.

"*Venus de Milo*," Nana guesses.

Lord Crawfish shakes his head no.

"The arm-y! You're joining the army?" Flora suggests.

"Armistice!" Vile blurts out. "Could it be that the war is over?"

Lord Crawfish smiles. It's true, he tells them. Finito. Kaput. No mas. Fin de la Guerre.

A celebration breaks out, and an eighth meal is served.

Downtrodden Abbey makes preparations for post-war life. The salon is gutted, as soldiers return to their homes and find

Edwardian tonsil hockey.

local hairdressers to accommodate their needs. Flora gently suggests to Marry that she give Atchew the boot and see if she can make it work with Calamine.

But just as he is about to leave, a miracle occurs. Atchew fully recovers the ability to speak (though his sexual function had suddenly diminished).

"It's incredible, Marry," he says. "I feel like I've never spoken before in my life. One takes for granted the simple, vocalised form of human communication—phonetic combinations of vowel and consonant sound units, which have formed the basis of thousand of languages over the centuries, and—"

"Blah, blah, blah! Atchew, I know you're excited about being able to speak again," Lady Marry says. "But do you think you could maybe, um . . . shut up for a bit?"

Lord Crawfish suffers some post-traumatic effects as he

realizes the toll that the war took, not just on Downtrodden Abbey but on all of England, and the world. So much senseless violence and killing. The coiffure-related needs of thousands of soldiers.

The despondent earl spends his evenings pacing the pantry, which is an uncomfortable area in which to pace, but holds the greatest likelihood of him encountering Jen, the object of his growing interest.

"Why, Lord Crawfish—what are you doing here?" Jen asks.

"More to the point," he answers, "What are *you* doing here?"

"I was just getting some flour," she explains, scratching her head. "You do realize that I am here often, right? I mean, fetching supplies is a big part of my job."

"Of course, of course. I suppose I am just a bit—nervous around you."

The earl makes a move towards the lowly housekeeper, then pretends he was reaching for a can of peaches. Jen backpedals, then acts as though she sees a mouse scurrying along the floor-boards. This causes Lord Crawfish to step to the side, where he examines a bag of rice. Jen then dusts a jam jar.

"Well, this is all a bit awkward," she says. "What do you suppose would happen if we just got it over with already and kissed?"

"How dare you suggest such a thing! I can have you dismissed immediately for merely uttering such distasteful words!"

"But Lord Crawfish—why would you loiter in the pantry and stare at me when I entered, if you had no secret agenda to encounter me?"

"All right, maybe just one little smooch," Lord Crawfish whispers. "Pucker up, Tootsie."

Atchew and Slovenia begin planning their wedding, which immediately presents a conflict between them, as she prefers a Victrola jockey, while he pleads for live music. Having selected a date, Lady Marry's and Calamine's nuptials get delayed. Which might not be a bad thing.

THE EDWARDIAN WEDDING

In the Edwardian Age, there was no more reported or anticipated event than a society wedding.

The process was slightly involved. Licenses were procured from the archbishop of Canterbury, whose office was open on Mondays from 9:00 a.m. to 10:30 a.m., and Wednesdays from 2 p.m. to 4:00 p.m. Unless the clerk was ill (she was prone to debilitating headaches), in which case the office was open on Saturdays from 11:00 a.m. to 1:30 p.m.

Once the license was obtained, the names of the wedding participants were required to be published for three successive weeks prior to the ceremony in the parish where the groom took residence, and five weeks in the district in which the bride lived.

Alternately, a marriage by license could be arranged. Applications for this type of license could be procured at the Vicar-General's office (for summer weddings), the Doctor's Commons (for winter weddings), or local apothecaries (for autumn weddings). The application then had to be completed, notarized, and posted to the Office of Civil Affairs, along with all appropriate fees.

The gown and trousseau worn by the bride had to meet certain specifications. For weekday weddings, creamy satin or almond was the preferred colour, whilst for weekend affairs, the bride was asked to wear ivory, vanilla, or beige. Veils were to be made of lace or tulle. Trains could be no more than ninety inches in length.

A typical gown was festooned with flounces of point d'Angelterre, with the court train attached at the shoulders and dropping to exactly three feet, two inches from the ground. The trim featured a border of daisies wrought with sequins and rubies, unless the bride was fair-skinned, in which case the flowers would be red carnations, wrought with emeralds and pearls. If the groom was over six inches taller than the bride, his hat could be not more than fourteen inches in height.

Perhaps due to the specifications of these requirements, double suicides of prospective brides and grooms were quite common.

Vile once again puts her nose where it does not belong. She notices that Marry breaks down crying every time the marriage of Slovenia and Atchew is mentioned, and corners her in the parlour.

"Don't tell me you're still in love with that bozo," says Vile, with as much sensitivity as she can muster.

"Look, I know he's a stooge, grandmother. But the heart wants what it wants."

Vile turns her attention to Atchew, in hopes that she can get him to change his mind. She tells him that Slovenia is nothing but a manipulative harlot who will only cause him emotional pain. That her thin, bony frame will quite possibly break if engaged in carnal activity. That she is unable to have children, strangely malodorous, and has been known to torture house-cats. And that rumours abound that Slovenia might in fact be the daughter of the evil Norse god Loki.

"Oh, Vile," counters Atchew. "She's really not that thin. It really depends on what she's wearing."

Calamine has his concerns that Atchew and Marry still have strong feelings for one another, so he does what any honour-able man would: he decides to have her tailed. He asks Nana to follow Marry's every move over a two-week period in order to determine her intentions.

"But, Mr. Calamine," Nana protests. "I'll be terminated. I have too many responsibilities here at Downtrodden."

"Silly girl. I can set you up for life. You'll have more toilet tissue at your disposal than you'll know what to do with."

Nana rats out Calamine to Tyresom, who is appalled that he even considered working for a man of such dubious charac-ter. Tyresom tells Lady Marry that he will not be accompanying her and Calamine to Hoare House.

Lady Marry is all, like, how dare you insult my future hus-band? And Tyresom is all, like, dude—what up with the atti-tude? I just thought you'd want to know. So Lady Marry is all, like, you're a really lousy butler anyway, everyone knows that. And Tyresom is all, like, you are so totally dead to me.

So Lady Marry is all, like, fine, whatever. (*Author's note: My thirteen-year-old niece wrote the previous paragraph. A little rough around the edges, but I think she's got some talent, don't you?*)

Brace confides to Nana that he prepared a dish containing rat poison and served it to Viral shortly before her death. He says he would tell the police, but he is afraid they might draw the wrong conclusions.

"But isn't that what you're saying—that you killed her?"

The veins in Brace's forehead bulge. "Nana, where would you ever get that idea? Do we live in so timid an age that trying new recipes is frowned upon? Why does everyone suspect me of wrongdoing? In fact, why does everyone in this whole bloody place suspect everyone else? Don't people realize that without some degree of compassion, we are doomed to a world of mistrust and backstabbing?"

Nana collects her thoughts before answering Brace's series of questions. "From what you said. Perhaps. Because of your expression. Wealthy people are bored and have nothing else to do. No."

Brace scowls. "Do you mean to tell me that you have never heard a rhetorical question before?"

"No, actually, I haven't—"

"—Nana, for God's sake. You need to just learn to *listen*."

"Let's get married, Mr. Brace."

"This is what I'm talking about! Didn't you hear a word I said? I'm about to be arrested, arraigned, tried, convicted, indicted, and incarcerated. Perhaps hanged! And not just for bad cooking—for murder. Do you really want to be wedded to someone who's been accused of murdering his first wife? *And* is a poor cook?"

Nana is silent.

"Well, do you?"

She grabs a writing tablet and scribbles: *Now I'm confused. Are these rhetorical questions?*

Handsom starts a group called Occupy Buckingham Palace, and encourages Lady Supple to run away with him and fight financial inequity. He feels that she can make no greater statement than to leave the comforts of Downtrodden Abbey for a life of greasy fish and chips, protests, dirty compatriots, rioting, and hastily created songs with grade-school lyrics and unlistenable melodies. Also, she has to sleep with an Irishman (*ugh*).

Supple must admit that Handsom makes the life he imagines sound awfully romantic. But she wonders if the destitute driver covets a partnership not due to her sharing his devotion to social change, but for her curvy waistline, ice-blue eyes, and full, sensual lips. She shares these feelings with him.

"Don't be silly, Supple. I know that underneath that smooth, silky skin and those raven tresses is a deeply committed fighter for economic parity. You cannot possibly feel content with the idea that some few have so much, while so many have so little."

"This is just a passing trend, Handsom," Lady Supple says. "I have no doubt that in a few short years the world's wealth will be spread. Hunger will be eradicated. And the only time we will hear about the 'one per cent' will be when individuals are purchasing low-fat milk."

Tomaine, meanwhile, continues to steal vinegar, which he sells to London's burgeoning underground world of artisanal chefs. Infusing the liquid with lavender, garlic, and the essence of orange blossoms, he leaves the Abbey after hours and trades his condiments illicitly on London's backroads, with merchants of ill repute. Within weeks, he becomes one of England's most notorious vinegar brokers, and there is hardly a salad or appetizer that has not been somehow touched by Tomaine's criminal hand.

The next night at dinner, Lady Supple is nowhere to be found. The drawing room is searched, and then the library.

"I thought I saw her with a rope, in the ballroom," says Enid. One dinner guest named Professor Plum suggests that she might have been struck with a spanner in the kitchen. Another, Colonel Mustard, firmly believes that a dagger in the lounge was Lady Supple's undoing. Miss Scarlett, another visitor, believes that a revolver she saw in the study was involved, while Mrs. Peacock is convinced that a lead pipe in the conservatory led to her murder.

"I think we might consider some other possibilities," says Lady Marry. "What if she ran away with that bleeding-heart driver, Handsom?"

"Why would they run when they can drive?" asks Enid, whose opinion, as usual, is ignored.

"I'll tell you one thing," Lord Crawfish snarls. "If Supple has taken off with that left-leaning jalopy jockey, she can forget about getting one pound of an inheritance from me. *Esto es un situación muy mal.*"

"Why, Roderick," Lady Flora says. "You're speaking Spanish."

Mrs. Used, the housekeeper, enters with a solemn expression. "I'm afraid I have a disheartening announcement to make. The Spanish flu has arrived in England. We'll all be speaking *Español* soon.

"I recommend that to avoid getting sick, we all eat as much of Mrs. Patmimore's chicken soup as we can."

The diners at the table eye one another disgustedly.

"Let me get this straight," Flora says. "You're suggesting that we ingest Mrs. Patmimore's cooking as a way to *prevent* illness?"

———

XII

Good Lord!

Three months have passed. The Spanish Flu has hit Countess Flora particularly hard, and she has taken to bed, where—because sleep is so difficult to come by—she plays the castanets and reads books about bullfighting incessantly.

Flora begins to worry for her life, and shares this concern with her husband.

"May I ask you a question, Roderick?"

"You just did, dear," Lord Crawfish responds.

"Seriously. I'll even try not to use the Spanish accent."

"Shoot."

Flora's eyes well up.

"If I perish, do you think you might remarry?"

Lord Crawfish considers this.

"Why, I might. I mean, I can only assume that you would want the best for me, Flora."

"Well . . . I would, but—would you, for example, let her wear my jewelry and furs?"

Lord Crawfish shrugs. "I suppose. I mean, if they were just sitting at your vanity and in your closet . . . would that be such a crime?"

"And would you allow her access to my gardening implements?"

"I don't see what the harm in that would be. With all due respect, they wouldn't do you much good in hel—in, uh, heaven." He smiles and puts his hand on hers.

"But, Roderick dear, would you . . . let her use my golf clubs?"

"Oh, absolutely not, don't you worry," he says. "I can assure you, with all certainty, that she is left-handed."

When Lord Crawfish hears of Lady Supple's intent to marry Handsom, he tracks the lowly driver down at a seedy pub.

"What would it take for you to never see my daughter again?" he asks.

"Buy me a drink," Handsom says.

Lord Crawfish is astounded. "That's all you need to call off your marriage to Supple? One drink?"

"Oh, Lord no, Lord," Handsom replies. "I have trouble hearing from that side. I thought you said, 'What do you want to drink along with that water, man?'"

"Look, Supple is the most wonderful woman I have ever known," he continues. "There probably isn't enough money in the Bank of England, Fort Knox, and Tomaine's pockets put together to keep us apart. Nonetheless, I would suggest you hire a lawyer, form a limited partnership, and start raising funds."

Feeling the anxiety of multiple weddings, an ailing wife, and a possible future Irish son-in-law engaging in extortion, Lord Crawfish starts spending more time in the darkened kitchen pantry, searching out his new obsession, Jen. Before long he has participated in a clandestine kiss he will not soon forget.

"Well, *that* was awkward," says a snippy, sarcastic and familiar voice, following the kiss. "not necessarily *bad*, but definitely awkward."

"Tomaine!" Lord Crawfish says, flicking on the light. "What in the name of his majesty the king are you doing here in the darkened kitchen pantry?"

"I can tell you what I am *not* doing," Tomaine says, his lip quivering. "I am absolutely not stealing vinegar and selling it on the

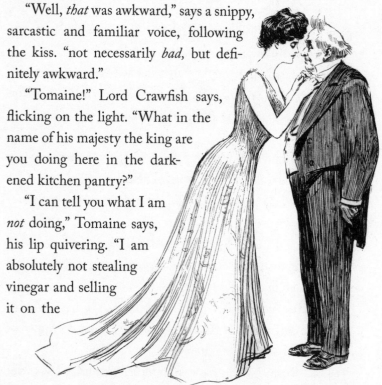

"Great wealth somehow masks the equine smell of an old man's breath."–Keats

"So what if I look like John Wilkes Booth? Shut up and kiss me!"

black market. Of that I am certain."

Lord Crawfish asks Tomaine why he would lay in wait for the chance to kiss him in the pantry.

"Oh, you have no idea where I'd *like* to kiss you," the footmasseur winks. "And by the way, what were *you* doing here? You can't put your trousers on without assistance, so it's unlikely that you were looking for ingredients to make yourself a midnight snack."

"I'm afraid that I have no choice but to fire you, Tomaine."

Slovenia is hit hard by the Spanish flu, and takes to bed. Atchew and Marry take the opportunity to enjoy some clandestine time together in the parlour.

"Should we 'canoodle' a bit?" Marry asks.

"There you go again with your big words," says Atchew. "In English, please. Olde, preferably."

"I just think it's time that we do more than flirt. We could cuddle, or share gentle touches, or—"

It is at this moment that Atchew makes the decision to shut

Marry and her impressive vocabulary up, in the simplest possible manner: he kisses her deeply. Music swells from the next room. And—this being Downtrodden Abbey, after all—this is the moment that Slovenia Swine comes down the stairs.

Slovenia wonders at first if her watery, puffy, Spanish flu-attacked eyes are deceiving her. She considers the possibilities. Perhaps Lady Marry had something on her lips that Atchew was helping her remove by using his mouth. Or maybe they were engaging in a staring contest, and merely got their faces closer than need be.

Slovenia startles the lovebirds. "Atchew!"

"Yes?" her intended responds.

"That was an actual sneeze, Atchew. Remember? I've been confined to my bed for several days."

Lady Marry approaches her. "You're not looking well, Slovenia. I think you should return to your quarters at once. Not that Atchew and I are trying to get rid of you or any-thing. Really. Go ahead. I'll come up and bring you a few magazines. Once I'm done, er, whatever I'm doing down here with Atchew. Which is nothing to worry about, just to recap."

Slovenia starts to suspect foul play as she heads back up-stairs.

By the next morning, she is dead. The medical examiner cites the cause of death as "Extreme heartbreak."

"Why, that's ridiculous," Vile, the dowager countess snorts. "It's not as if she is a character in a tawdry melodrama. *Heartbreak* is not a medical term."

This hardly assuages Lady Marry and Atchew's guilt as they attend Slovenia's funeral.

"Well, *this* is depressing," Atchew mutters, as he stands with Marry behind the other mourners. "It probably doesn't help that it's raining, a dirge is playing, we're all wearing black, and we're in England."

He grabs Marry and kisses her deeply.

"Atchew. We are at the funeral of your fiancée. This would be a good time to exert some measure of control over yourself."

Roderick is surprised to see that Lady Supple has attended the service with Handsom, who dresses appropriately but brings a sign protesting the use of the cemetery for what he calls "Human Landfill." Supple pleads with him not to picket the service.

"Honestly, Handsom—it's always something with you."

"You don't see me 'protesting' when you hold me next to your shapely, sensual curves," says the driver in his own defense.

Supple melts. "At least you have the quick wit so blatantly missing in most bleeding-heart liberals. Oh, yeah—and a particularly large penis."

Back at Downtrodden Abbey, dinner is disrupted by the appearance of Scotland Yard. Answering the door, Tyresom wonders how it's possible that a large piece of land has travelled to the estate; it is explained to him that Scotland Yard is actually the name used for the British police force. When he asks why it's not called "England Yard," he is shuttled into the next room, as Roderick interacts with the police inspector.

"I am here to arrest John Brace on counts of inferior cooking and intent to murder his wife, Viral. Oh, yeah—and of actually murdering her."

Tyresom explains that Brace is downstairs in the servant's quarters, and suggests that they come back in a few hours, at which time the valet may have navigated said stairs.

"What's this?" asks Nana, entering the foyer.

"It's a police inspector," Tyresom informs her. "This is Mr. Brace's fiancée," he informs the police inspector. *This is a disaster*, he informs himself.

"That's not what I mean. I mean, 'what's the meaning of this?' is what I mean."

The inspector explains to Nana that it might be a good time to rethink the idea of marrying John Brace. Or, at the very least, having him make her dinner if they do get married. But the truth is, where he's going, she won't have much to worry about either way.

"My God!" Lady Marry exclaims, as the police cart Brace away. "Do you know where they're taking him? Jail. Prison. The big house. The hoosegow. The stir. The brig. The clink. The rock. The pokey. The slammer. The stockade. The castle. The cooler. The joint. The hole. The farm. The sneezer. The stockade. The Greybar Hotel. Con college. He's going up the river. Up north."

After a British policemen complained about being called "Sally," the nickname "Bobby" was adopted.

"Marry, you have *got* to stop doing that," Vile demands, then points at the winsome wordsmith and asks the inspector, "Say, do you think perhaps you could take her as well?"

The roof of Downtrodden Abbey is removed every winter for the annual lowering in of the Christmas tree. Somehow the spirit of the season is slightly diminished this year. Perhaps it is due to John Brace's arrest and transport to prison, where he awaits sentencing for the murder of his wife. Or maybe it's the breakup of Atchew and Lady Marry, who is now convinced that marrying Dick Calamine is the answer to her and her family's problems. Or Tomaine, who has been welcomed back to the Abbey, but refused the position as Lord Crawfish's valet until he has replaced all of the vinegar he has stolen from the pantry.

Nana decides that a trip to Cockswallow, the prison housing her intended, could not possibly be more depressing than staying at the Abbey. Her journey to the institution takes three days. Brace tell her that the conditions are ghastly, and that he is constantly mocked for his disability. Nana tries to cheer him up.

"Look at the bright side, John," says says. "You're around men you can bond with. You can catch up on your reading. You are getting three square meals a day."

"Thanks, Nana," says Brace. "Somehow I feel even worse now."

Back in the library at Downtrodden, Calamine starts to worry that Lady Marry is dragging her heels on setting a wedding date. She claims that she's in a sewing circle on Mondays, Tuesdays and Thursdays she's all about working out,

Wednesday night is book club, and the weekends are taken with polo and social events.

"You seem completely booked," Calamine moans.

"Oh, I'm sure she'll be able to fit you in," a voice says from behind. It is Lord Crawfish, who winks at Lady Marry as he speaks. "Lady Marry has such strong feelings for you, Dick, that she is just looking for the perfect day."

"Sometimes I wonder if you are interested in marrying me for less than honourable reasons," Calamine says.

"Not at all," says Lord Crawfish, whom Calamine thought had left the room. "Lady Marry is deeply in love with you. She particularly likes the feel of your hand on hers, the whisper of your soft breath, and the way your heart seems to race in her presence."

"Lord Crawfish!" the appalled Calamine barks. "You've pulled a book of Keats poetry off of the shelf and are reading from it! And Lady Marry seems to have slithered out of the room several minutes ago."

"Ah. You're so right. Please forgive me," says the Earl of Grandsun, before slithering out as well, leaving Calamine with his conflicted feelings.

On a regular basis, people are either eavesdropping or slithering in this place, he thinks. *What* up *with that?*

Upstairs, Lord Crawfish starts to question whether his daughter should marry Calamine after all. Flora sits him down for a talk.

"Roderick," she begins. "I'm going to break a basic law of dramatic writing and tell you something that anyone who might be watching already knows.

"Do you remember Camel, the Arab who stayed at Down-trodden Abbey last year? I'm afraid he . . . soiled Marry's sheets *and* reputation."

Lord Crawfish moans. "Oh, God, no."

"It's true, dearest. And Calamine's threatened to blackmail her."

"Then there's only one solution, Flora."

"And what's that?"

"I'm not sure. But I do know one thing—that there's only one solution. I think."

The Crawfishes retain a lawyer, Bernie, to help with the case involving Roderick's dear old friend Brace. None of the family has had much experience with Jews, but there is concern that Atchew—who is also an attorney—would have made a mess of things. For several days before meeting with Bernie, they practice drinking less and getting into even more trivial arguments than usual.

"I gotta be honest, it's not looking good," Bernie tells the Crawfishes. "Between that gimpy *schlemiel* starting up a thing with the maid—although believe me I understand, having seen her delicious *punim*—and then the *mishegas* with Brace going back to London, and the *farkakta* rat poison, it looks like you've got a real *magilla* on your hands."

Roderick and Flora look at each other and shrug. Though they don't understand a word Bernie says, they trust that they are in capable hands as the date of Brace's trial approaches.

Lady Enid goes missing, and Tomaine suggests that Down-trodden residents stage a massive hunt for her. They refuse.

Tomaine "finds" Enid, who tells everyone that it was he who kidnapped her in the first place, hid her in the doghouse, and planned to be a hero and ingratiate himself with Lord Crawfish by serving as her rescuer.

Instead, he is fired yet again.

XIII

Renewal (?)

A s the season winds down at Downtrodden Abbey—
and again, no one is exactly sure what "the Season"
is—the winds of fortune shift. Unable to tolerate
Calamine's threats to expose Lady Marry's sordid past, Atchew
slips him an exploding cigar. Humilated, Calamine flees, his
face ashen.

At Cockswallow Prison, John Brace gets a call from the
governor, who insists on being called "Guv'na." Brace is reluc-
tant to get on the phone, until someone explains to him what
"a call from the governor" means. He is granted a reprieve. And
after someone else clarifies what a "reprieve" is (he thought it
was when they repeat a song in a musical revue), Brace finally
understands that he may soon walk away as a free man. (Walk
with considerable difficulty, of course, but as a free man. So
he's got that going for him, which is good.)

Exploding cigars ushered in the first era of cosmetic surgery.

The Schleppers' Dance, an annual tradition at Downtrodden which had been cancelled due to the war, is rescheduled and held in high style. As this follows what is referred to as "awards season," the residents feel "renewed," and ready for another year of "episodes."

Roderick slow waltzes with Flora, as their love is rekindled in the wake of his near-miss affair with Jen. Tomaine is rehired, as the event desperately needs a choreographer. Even Lady Supple and Handsom make an appearance, if only to protest the drawn-out manner in which Atchew and Lady Marry have conducted their flirtation. Clearly, they are running out of things to protest.

Speaking of the on-again, off-again couple, Atchew chooses his moment to reach for Marry's arm, march her to the front of the Downtrodden Abbey ballroom, take a knee, and declare his eternal love for her.

In the decades before cellular phones, impatience was a scourge.

Again, he asks for her hand in marriage. Again, she misinterprets the expression and he must explain that it means more than just her hand. Again, Lord Roderick Crawfish and his wife worry for the future of their family and—more importantly—their fortune.

And then they hear Lady Marry utter these magic words in response to Atchew's proposal:

"You know what? Let me think about it."

Music swells, as do bits of Atchew. Credits roll.

Part Three

Being the Third of Three Parts

XIV

House of Mirthlessness

Flora Crawfish loves her mother, Surly McPain. She is just not at all certain if she *likes* her. Sometimes she thinks she likes the *idea* of her more than her actual being.

Which is all to say that Surly is pretty much a walking narcissistic personality disorder, and a monumental pain in the ass.

Journeying from her home in Sedona, Arizona, Surly arrives at Downtrodden for the wedding of Marry and Atchew. In short order, she begins to rant about Britain and its failings.

"You people think you invented the English muffin!" she snorts at dinner. "But it was the Scottish—the McDonalds, in fact—who deserve the credit. They popularized the so-called English muffin in the States, and we Americans figured how to eat them properly—with an egg in the middle, covered with cheese, and special sauce. Served between seven and eleven in the morning."

Vile winces at the mere thought.

"Can I ask you a question, Surly? What exactly are you doing here? We are concerned that your appearance at this wedding is a mere stunt, designed to increase attendance."

Surly can handle such criticism. She has endured far worse. A career in Hollywood films, for example. And a brother whose antics in the boudoir routinely made headlines. In fact, she believes that this is not her first physical incarnation. You know how someone will tell you that they think they were Joan of Arc, or Napoleon, in a former life? And you think, *yeah—right—sure you were!* Well, Surly makes a pretty convincing argument. She really does believe that she has previously led several lives. And she claims she's managed to get book deals to recount each and every one of them.

Her relentless yammering is interrupted by the arrival of Supple and Handsom, the latter of whom proves, in terms of patriotric fervor, to be even more obnoxious than Surly.

"The Irish—now *they* know breakfast. Leather-like bacon? That's us. Black pudding *and* white pudding? Check. Liver—why not? And of course, our signature contribution to the first meal of the day—baked beans!"

"Honestly," says Enid, "I think I'm going to be sick. Isn't it considered deplorable form to discuss breakfast when one is at dinner?"

This comment triggers another boast from Surly about how Americans also revolutionized poor table manners.

At the head of the table, Lord Crawfish can barely hear

this blather over the noise in his own head. Crawfish has recently learned that his investment of Flora's fortune—in a chain of Big & Tall Men's clothing shops in Tokyo—has been a massive mistake.

Marry intervenes, threatening to withhold her affection from Atchew if he refuses to do one little favor for her—keep Downtrodden Abbey in the family.

"Withhold your affection? You mean, you would refuse to marry me, Marry?"

"Oh, no, I didn't say that," she assures him. "Technically, we *would* be married. I would just ignore you, make sure that my interests don't intersect with yours, and keep my communication limited."

"Oh, Marry, my sweet, naïve thing. That *is* marriage!"

The wedding is an extravagant affair, during which some less-than-extravagant affairs are carried on in the upstairs bedrooms, the pantry, and the barn (don't ask).

When Surly is solicited for the funds to save Downtrodden, she has no choice but to sneak off and return to America.

Edsel Parks was one of the military salon's finest colorists when she got—how to put this delicately—knocked up by one of the soldiers. Forced to give up the child, she turned to opium, developed an addiction, and became a prostitute.

"Not the most impressive curriculum vitae," says Vile. Nonetheless, Edsel is hired as a scullery maid, against the wishes of the dowager countess.

"Is it that difficult to find someone to scrub carrots?" Vile asks.

"The girl really has a knack," shrugs Isabich.

Meanwhile, Enid begins a torrid hand-holding relationship with Sir Antonio Stallion, who is not only a crippled geriatric, but is one of Marry's castoffs. Flora is unhappy about their blooming relationship.

"Enid," she warns. "Look at Nana. A young girl like that, saddled with an accused murderer who goes to prison, threatened regularly by violent cellmates, and—"

"—All right, Mother. You're making me jealous."

"Jealous?!? Of Nana's miserable existence?"

"She's *married*," Enid explains. "I mean, how long do you think I can go, with this face and personality, before my chances of finding a life partner are permanently dashed?"

Good point, Flora thinks.

"Oh, don't be silly, darling," Flora says. "You have a big, long life ahead of you. Women don't expire until they reach their forties these days."

Atchew receives a letter saying that he is being left a small fortune. He suspects that it is from a Nigerian prince. (It just has that vibe, you know?)

Rarely solicited prostitute.

"Darling, don't be a stooge," says his loving new bride, Marry. "It's from the late father of Slovenia Swine."

Slovenia Swine . . . Slovenia Swine, thinks Atchew.

Marry reminds Atchew that Slovenia was the former fiancée, whom he dumped unceremoniously. Though she is dead, Marry believes that there is an opportunity for Atchew to take further advantage of her if he so desires—to take every shilling of her late father's estate. And in doing so, save Downtrodden Abbey by handing the money to Lord Crawfish.

"So it's victory-victory, all the way," Marry adds.

Upon hearing Atchew's offer, however, Lord Crawfish almost turns down the gift.

"I've actually been looking at a big two-bedroom in the village," he explains.

"Roderick, are you mad?" scoffs Atchew. "You have a forty-person staff, a wife, and grown children to house. Don't let your pride get the best of you."

The morning of Enid's wedding day arrives. The hopeful bride begins to get worried when she sees that no one has responded to the invitation, sent a gift, or visited the registry (by standing) online at Boudoirs, Bath & Beyond.

Nonetheless, she dresses for the event and—for her—actually doesn't look too unfortunate. But that's not enough to deter Sir Stallion, who leaves a dashed-off note at the altar that reads, "Um . . . sorry. I had some stuff to do."

Enid is devastated. She cannot even get a commitment from an infirmed, aged, malodorous loser.

Tomaine finds himself bored for a few hours and decides to spread a rumour about O'Grotten. He settles on a bad case of the crabs, but the scheme backfires when O'Grotten is given a week off and sent flowers and gifts.

With her three-year contract at Downtrodden running out, he prays that she doesn't renew it.

XV

Irish Stupor

After returning to Dublin, Handsom starts working as a fry cook in a small town. (After this is discovered, he is formally hired by the establishment.) But when he burns the toast of a local aristocrat, the restaurant's particularly punitive manager calls the police. Handsom is pursued to the border; in a panicked fit of self-hatred, he heads to Downtrodden Abbey.

"Where is Supple?" asks Marry.

"I knew I forgot something," Handsom replies sheepishly.

"How could you, Handsom? She's with child!"

"No, she's not . . . she's alone!" He thinks for a moment. "Wait, does 'with child' mean . . . pregnant?"

In prison, Brace has not heard from Nana in weeks. Her letters to him have been intercepted by the warden and adapted as a musical by the Cockswallow Theatre Ensemble. Sadly, Brace learns of this when he attends the opening, and the lead—a male prisoner, in drag—belts out a song entitled "Don't Call My Husband a Lowly Cripple, He's Also an Accused Murderer." (It was the warden's first attempt as a librettist, and it goes without saying that his work subsequently improved.)

Back at Downtrodden, Tyresom hires a new footmasseur, Jiggy, who immediately turns the heads of both male and female residents and staff members.

"Your job is not the turning of heads," Tyresom admonishes him. "It is the massaging of the feet."

Prison theatre dance number.

Meanwhile, a comely blonde, Hivy, is recruited as a scullery maid. Laizy gives her a hero's welcome by bitching her out every chance she gets.

Enid—who has barely survived a nervous breakdown following her jilting at the altar—begins to develop not just stress-related cold sores, but progressive political beliefs. These manifest in nightly walks around Downtrodden, during which she incessantly makes birdlike sounds. When Marry asks what she is doing, Enid replies, "Why, I'm tweeting, of course."

Marry suggests that rather than tweeting, Enid express herself in a more modern fashion such as the telegraph, or a newspaper column.

Atchew approaches Marry warily in the drawing room.

"Sorry to interrupt your drawing," he says. "But . . . I need to talk to you about your father."

"Ohmigod," Marry gasps, dropping her charcoal. "Don't tell me he's been kissing some young maid behind the stable . . . and he's leaving my mother . . . and taking off with this girl somewhere into the Midlands . . . never to be heard from again—"

"Marry, get a grip," Atchew says, stroking her wrist. "I just wanted to raise the possibility that Roderick may . . . not be so good with money."

Marry turns away from him. "How dare you malign my father's character like that! This from someone who a few short years ago was eating fish with a grapefruit spoon!"

"You know what?" Atchew moans. "Forget I said anything."

Atchew has become increasingly aware of Marry's extreme

mood swings of late. He has also noticed a protrusion of her lower stomach area. She has been vomiting in the mornings, and eating odd combinations of food.

He would think she was pregnant, if he knew any better.

No such luck.

Supple, meanwhile, has a veritable "labour party," as anyone and everyone seems to be present for her and Handsom's blessed event—the arrival of Lord Grandsun's first grandchild. When Supple suffers complications, the dunderheaded earl arranges for a medical face-off. The diagnosticians in question are the kindly, caring doctor who has known the Crawfish family for decades, and an obnoxious obstetrician whose sole claim to fame is that he served as Roscoe "Fatty" Arbuckle's nutritionist.

Guess who wins?

Supple can tell you.

Actually, sadly . . . she cannot.

Unlicensed family doctors often prescribed "Lox, bagels, and a schmear."

XVI

—⊶⊷⊙⊶⊷—

Supple Differences

Handsom is further chastised by Flora for the name he chooses for the baby.

"'Supple'? Really? Seriously inappropriate," she barks.

"But you named *your* daughter that . . ." Handsom responds.

Times were different, the countess thinks. *Women weren't just considered bodies in bustiers back then. Hopefully, though, with the increasing popularity of motion pictures, that will all change. Women will be looked at in entirely new ways, not just as sexual objects. And who knows? Perhaps they will even make significant inroads in the areas of directing, producing, and screenwriting! Which reminds me—I have got to get back to my script . . .*

When she comes out of her reverie and faces Handsom, he is gone.

Blaming Roderick for Supple's death seems to infuse Flora with energy, and provides a nifty excuse for sleeping in a separate bedroom.

Edsel, the former prostitute, is assigned the daunting task of preparing lunch for the Crawfish women. Mrs. Patmimore admonishes her to leave her old life behind as she presents each course.

"'Ow 'bout a date, then?" Edsel says, proffering the starter, a dish of plump Moroccan Medjools. "Who of you lot would like to join me for a date? Guarantee you've

Inexperienced waitstaff often covered their anxiety with blank stares.

never sampled sweet flesh like this, guv'nahs . . ."

Overhearing this from the kitchen, Mrs. Patmimore hits herself over the head with a meat tenderizer.

At Cockswallow, Brace meets a Jewish inmate, Maurie, and asks him if he is, by any chance, a lawyer. As luck would have it he is, and after reviewing his fellow prisoner's case, he approaches Brace in the chow hall.

"I think I've found a loophole," Maurie whispers.

"Best way to keep your trousers up," says Brace.

Oy, this guy is always with the schtick, thinks Maurie.

"No, *bubelah*—I mean a loophole in your *farkakta* situation.

With the wife, and the cooking, and the murder, and the blaming. I think I can get you sprung, *boychik*. You'll be back in the McMansion *schtupping* your little chambermaid in no time."

Though he fervently wishes that his attorney were less of a cultural stereotype, Brace is granted an . . . er, *exodus* from Cockswallow.

But as pleased as he may be upon his release from prison, it only triggers more from Tomaine's bottomless pit of resentment; that the gimpy murder suspect—rather than he—will again be holding Lord Crawfish's trousers, provoked his rage.

It is, perhaps, this venom that sends him to Jiggy's bedroom, where he plants a wet one on the succulent-but-unsuspecting lips of the sleeping footmasseur. (That and O'Grotten, who claims that Jiggy has been quoting Oscar Wilde incessantly lately, and taking needlepoint lessons.)

"Tomaine!" Jiggy screams. "When I flutter my eyelashes at you, I am doing it *ironically*! And I've only been grabbing your rump because I've heard you keep loose change in your back pocket. What kind of perv do you think I am, man?"

"What are you accusing me of?" asks Tomaine.

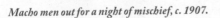

Macho men out for a night of mischief, c. 1907.

"Well, how about answering a question with a question, for starters?"

"Aren't you one to talk?"

"I don't know, am I?"

And so it went. (Or did it?)

Though Supple's death and Handsom's vow to raise the child as a Buddhist is gracious plenty to put the Grandsuns in a tizzy, it is an announcement by Enid that finally sends them over the edge.

"It's official. I'm going into journalism!" she declares at dinner.

"Oh, Enid. Darling, how can throw your life away like this? There was a reporter who did a story on Downtrodden a few years ago. They said that we were upstanding, generous, compassionate souls who give back to the community and treat our help as though they were family."

"Yes, I know, father—they got everything wrong. That's what I want to change! I want to make a difference, like Supple did. Affect social reform. Expose evil, and analyze ways to repair trouble and turmoil."

Vile, the dowager countess, is so stirred to respond that she actually stands up. "We Crawfish have never been in the business of repairing turmoil," she snorts. "We *create* it."

XVII

Don't Think and Drive

Any opportunity to soil white clothing and make the servants' lives even more miserable is an open door for the Crawfish family. And the annual rugby match is just such an opportunity.

What's at stake this year is Atchew's future with the family. He has been an active "cast" member, shall we say, at Down-trodden for three years. Marry and the others have been fairly certain that his commitment is solid. But the fact that Atchew has brought an agent, Howie Kreplach, to the rugby game—and that they are playing for the other team—seems rather suspect, to say the least.

"Surely you can stick around for another season," Lord Crawfish tells Atchew on the sidelines between scrums.

"I've got other things I want to do," Atchew explains.

"Maybe Atchew wants to live with another family for a

while," says Kreplach. "And, I mean nothing's definite, but he is entertaining other offers."

Lord Crawfish considers this preposterous. A man with a pregnant wife considering other options?

"Look," he says, trying to calm the situation before the next play. "I'll be the first to admit—I'm weak. I exemplify old money, I prey on young housemaids, and I am terrible at business.

"You, on the other hand, are young and handsome. You've all but saved Downtrodden from ruin. You'd be desperately missed if your agent lets you go to another, er . . . family."

Atchew is touched by Roderick's candor.

"Let me think about it this afternoon," he says. "I'm going on a high-speed automobile ride on a narrow, curvy road. It'll be the perfect time for me to wrap my head around a tree."

Roderick looks at him.

"What?"

"I mean, the *situation*," Atchew says. "To wrap my head around the *situation*."

Life goes on at Downtrodden Abbey. Roderick and Flora reconcile. Mrs. Patmimore gets involved with a man who finds her buns irresistible—but sadly for her, only in the literal sense. At the county fair Tomaine saves Jiggy's butt, but that's as close to Jiggy's butt as he is allowed. Marry's baby is born.

As for Atchew?

Let us just say that—as far as living is concerned—his contract is up.

HISTORICAL INACCURACY
THE CREATION AND
DEVELOPMENT OF THE
DOWNTRODDEN ABBEY SERIES
AND PRODUCTION NOTES

While *Downtrodden Abbey* is a work of fiction, great pains have been taken to adhere closely to the facts of Edwardian life early in the twentieth century. The estate itself is based on Lowdownne Castle, which was built in the 1700s but—despite being made of stone—was destroyed by an infestation of particularly aggressive termites.

Though cosmetic surgery was uncommon in the time in which *Downtrodden* is set, the producers found it near to impossible to cast even one actor who had not had some work done.

This series has proven to be a tremendous challenge in the areas of budget, casting, and supervision of period detail, and in the interest of historical accuracy, the producers would like to acknowledge the following errors. We regret these anachronisms and will make best efforts to have them removed for the inevitable expensive boxed set planned for Christmas release after the series has finally run its course.

maine, the footmasseur, has a tattoo of the pop singer Harry Connick
. on his left shoulder, which is visible in Episode 4 of Season One. Harry
Connick Jr. was born in 1967. We have arranged for this image to be
digitally replaced with an overlay of Beatrice Lillie, a saucy dance hall
performer of the day.

. In Episode 2 of Season Two, Atchew is seen at breakfast drinking from a
can of Red Bull. Contrary to rumours on the Internet, Red Bull—the
most popular energy drink in the world with sales of 4.5 billion units per
year—was not involved in the financing or partial underwriting of *Downtrodden Abbey*. However, we would like to point out that Red Bull mixes
wonderfully with many alcohol-based products, provides midday stimu-
lation at the workplace, and tastes great over ice. Red Bull gives you
wings! Look for it at your local grocer or beverage supply store.

3. Lady Enid is rather conspicuously fiddling with an iPhone at the Schlep-
per's Dance, in the conclusion of Season Two. We have received an apol-
ogy from the actor who portrays Lady Enid, who was evidently "tweeting"
her feelings about the breakup of Tom Cruise and Katie Holmes. We
would like to further extend our regrets to the famous couple, who we
really believed had a shot, were it not for the cutthroat tabloid media
and their excesses, not to mention the pressure of living in the public eye.

4. Tyresom sports a button on his left lapel in Season Three's fifth episode that reads "Stop Fracking Now." During filming, the producers
believed that this was a historically accurate statement that condemned
what they mistook for a colloquialism for "fornication." In truth, fracking
is indeed slang for Hydraulic Fracturing, which involves multiple frac-
tures of rock layer by pressurized fluid as a means to access and release
natural gas or petroleum.

Fracking enthusiasts believe that once inaccessible hydrocarbons ex-
tracted through this activity create substantial financial benefits to oil
companies and consumers. Those opposed to the process are quick to expose the ecological toll, including air pollution and groundwater con-
tamination. (The producers of *Downtrodden Abbey* have taken no public
position on this issue, and staunchly defend the rights of individual viewers to exercise and voice their own opinions.)

5. In Episode 3 of Season Two, astute viewers may notice that the chauffeur, Handsom, is driving a 2012 Kia Sedona Minivan. The producers regret this oversight, which again in no way reflects the economic challenges of mounting an expensive period drama. In their defense, they do firmly believe that *if* Handsom were to time-travel and be offered his choice of ground transport vehicles, Kia's line of luxurious but affordable sedans, station wagons, SUVs, and minivans would be an obvious choice. Proud recipient of a five-star crash safety rating, the Sedona features a rear seat DVD entertainment system with wireless headsets and remote control— whatever your family needs for anything from a drive to school to a drive across the country. New thinking. New possibilities. Only from Kia.

6. Starting with Season Two, O'Grotten occasionally expresses her irritation and disappointment by employing the phrase "Whatevs." "Whatevs" is a shortened form of the colloquialism "Whatever," which is meant to convey these thoughts: *Whatever you say, I don't care what you say,* or *I do not think what you are saying is relevant.* It was popularized in California's San Fernando Valley in the 1980s, and—though there is no evidence— the likelihood is slim that "Whatevs" was used regularly during the Edwardian Age.

7. While Flora is an American character, her tendency to hum the theme song from *Gilligan's Island* while in the bath is unsupported by period research. *Gilligan's Island* aired on the CBS television network from 1964 to 1967. To this day, the debate rages on amongst American males as to who was more attractive, Ginger or Mary Ann. It is unlikely to be resolved anytime soon, and the producers of *Downtrodden Abbey* are divided in their opinions. While no one would argue that Ginger is an alluring sexpot, Mary Ann has the fresh-faced enthusiasm of the proverbial "girl next door."

8. Mr. Brace's self-diagnosis of restless leg syndrome is simply a load of crap, as is Nana's claim that she suffers from Epstein-Barr virus. Certainly didn't stop them from meeting up regularly and canoodling behind the stable, did it?

9. In the Arbor Day episode, Fodder's suggestion that the residents of Downtrodden Abbey participate in "a lively game of Quidditch" is a blatant attempt to cash in on the success of J. K. Rowling's Harry Potter books.

BIBLIOGRAPHY

Pardon Me, But Your Finger Is in My Nostril: A Guide to Edwardian Etiquette, Devon Cornpipe, Stuffed Veal Breast Publications, 1932.

"This Scullery Is Bloody Filthy" and Other Thoughts of a Working Maid, Elizabeth Corset-Stretching, Regurgitation Books, 1928.

The Tramp's Tramps: The Love Life of Charlie Chaplin, Leonard Malted-Milkball, Skidmark University Press, 1983.

Oh, Fork it! The Ultimate Cutlery Book, Randolph Puckstone, Flying Wombat/Sulking Panda Books, 1951.

Cooking Blind: Recipes and Safety Tips, Finola Gardenshears, No Such Thing as Bad Press, 1947.

The Oxford Encyclopaedia of Prosthetic Limbs, Spartacus Futon III, Bench Press, 1862.

Backwards, March! A History of Meaningless British Protests Over Trivial Issues, Bryce Cottonmouth, Thunderous Wind Publications, 1968.

If the King Had Balls . . ., Alexandra Sickbed-Colitis, Kornhauser Books, 1991.

I Find Virtually Everything Unacceptable, Distasteful, Unsatisfactory, or Re-

volting: The Diary of a Dowager Countess, Dowager Countess Judith
Deertick-Van Diesel, Unread Books, 1924.

Pantywaists and Punjabs: The Sexual Politics of England and India, text by
Winston Salem, illustrations by Virginia Slims, Hardcourt & Tweezers,
1957.

ACKNOWLEDGEMENTS

I must take this opportunity to thank the individuals who made it possible to produce this volume is such a timely and efficient manner, as well as those who have strongly intimated that they should be mentioned, and the few who have already prepared to begin legal proceedings lest I cite them as valuable, indispensible participants.

First and foremost, I would like to thank my editor, Regina Muddpak, who inspired me when I was anxious or procrastinating by making herself completely unavailable. This unusual strategy motivated me to push on with writing even as I continued calling her, emailing her, and privately wondering if she had entered the Witness Protection Program. My thanks for the silent support. Regina's assistant, Scott Feathers, took full advantage of her absence with his own lack of visibility or efficiency. I believe a full editor position is in his future.

My research assistant, Alexander Cranberry, proved to be an indispensible resource on the subject of Edwardian manners, despite an ironic personal void in that department. Every time I see a dirty dish left on a desk, a water stain or cigarette burn on a piece of expensive furniture, or the contents of an unflushed commode, I will see Alexander's face. And flush that toilet with gusto.

The designer of this book, Florinda Mallard-Carkas, inadvertently served as the descendant of *Downtrodden Abbey*'s legally blind chef, Mrs. Patmimore. Enough said, I believe.

Marcus Robertson is a literary agent for the ages—and the aged. I have been waiting for him to retire for decades, but at the ripe age of ninety-seven, he is still going strong(ish). Marcus's hearing aid evidently was acting up during negotiations with the publisher, and he ended up getting me considerably less money for this book than originally estimated. I hope he is able to hear the proceedings when I begin my litigation against him.

Many of you may have read that my long-term marriage to Clarabelle Winchester took its toll during the extraordinary journey that led to this book's publication. However, I would like to clear up some of the rumours that have emerged in the tabloids on this subject:

1. Clarabelle's comments in the *Daily Mail* that I am a "lonely, tortured megalomaniac" with "a severe personality disorder" and "incapable of giving or returning affection" were, I believe, taken out of context. Keep in mind that this is a woman who has been medicated since the age of eleven.

2. In any event, who is she to talk? I pay for tennis lessons, and she ends up going away for a weekend to a "tournament" with her instructor? Tell me that isn't a bald-faced violation of the sacred contract of marriage.

3. I am not, nor have ever been, a cross-dresser. I did happen to attend a party celebrating the opening of the Meryl Streep film *The Iron Lady*, for which I was informed that the attendees were requested to be costumed as Prime Minister Margaret Thatcher. I have reason to believe that Clarabelle not only put me up to this reprehensible stunt, but made sure that there was extensive cell phone photography and video coverage of my entrance.

4. Not to engage in petty mudslinging, but anyone with Google Images can see that Clarabelle's weight has really ballooned since she left me. Save some ice cream for the rest of the world, Toots!

5. Anyone interested in taking tennis lessons should by all means avoid engaging the services of Brian Winslow. He has a 3.5 player rating, at best, and has never made the finals of any significant British tournaments. Your local club will be happy to furnish you with a list of tennis pros in your area, one of whom will undoubtably fit your needs.

Lastly, I would like to thank the men and women who lived and worked at Lowdownne Castle, which served as the inspiration for *Downtrodden Abbey*. As a child, I was fascinated by the stories I would hear about the class struggles, affairs, jealousy, deception, illegal abortions, murder, and bad food that pervaded early twentieth-century England.

Later, I thought it might make for a delightful and entertaining diversion. It is my fervent wish that you, the reader, agree.

Gillian Fetlocks
December, 2013

INDEX

ABOUT THE AUTHOR

Gillian Fetlocks is the latest pseudonym for Billy Frolick, whose bestselling parodies include *The Ditches of Edison County* (as Ronald Richard Roberts), *The Philistine Prophecy* (as McCoy Hatfield), and *The Five People You Meet in Hell* (as Rich Pablum). His screenwriting credits include DreamWorks Animation's *Madagascar,* which has spawned two sequels, a stage production, a television series, and a line of Pez dispensers.

Frolick's writing has appeared in *The New Yorker,* Salon.com, and *The Los Angeles Times.* He is at work on a novel about a man who gets younger with each successive romantic encounter, tentatively titled *Fifty Shades of Dorian Gray.*